A Walk Through Tears

A Walk Through Tears

ONE OF THE GREATEST MIRACLES IN MODERN TIMES

New and updated edition

Dot Roberts with Dr. Ricky Roberts

A WALK THROUGH TEARS by Dot Roberts
With Dr. Ricky Roberts

Unless otherwise noted, the Scripture quotations are from The King James Version of the Bible.
Scripture quotations marked NKJV are from the New King James Version of the Bible.

Library of Congress Control Number: 2003105731
International Standard Book Number: 1-59185-236-6
This book was previously published by Dr. Ricky Roberts, ISBN 0-8187-0347-4, copyright © 2001 and 2003.
03 04 05 06 8 7 6 5 4 3 2 1
Printed in the United States of America
ISBN 13: 9781542818650
ISBN 10: 1542818656

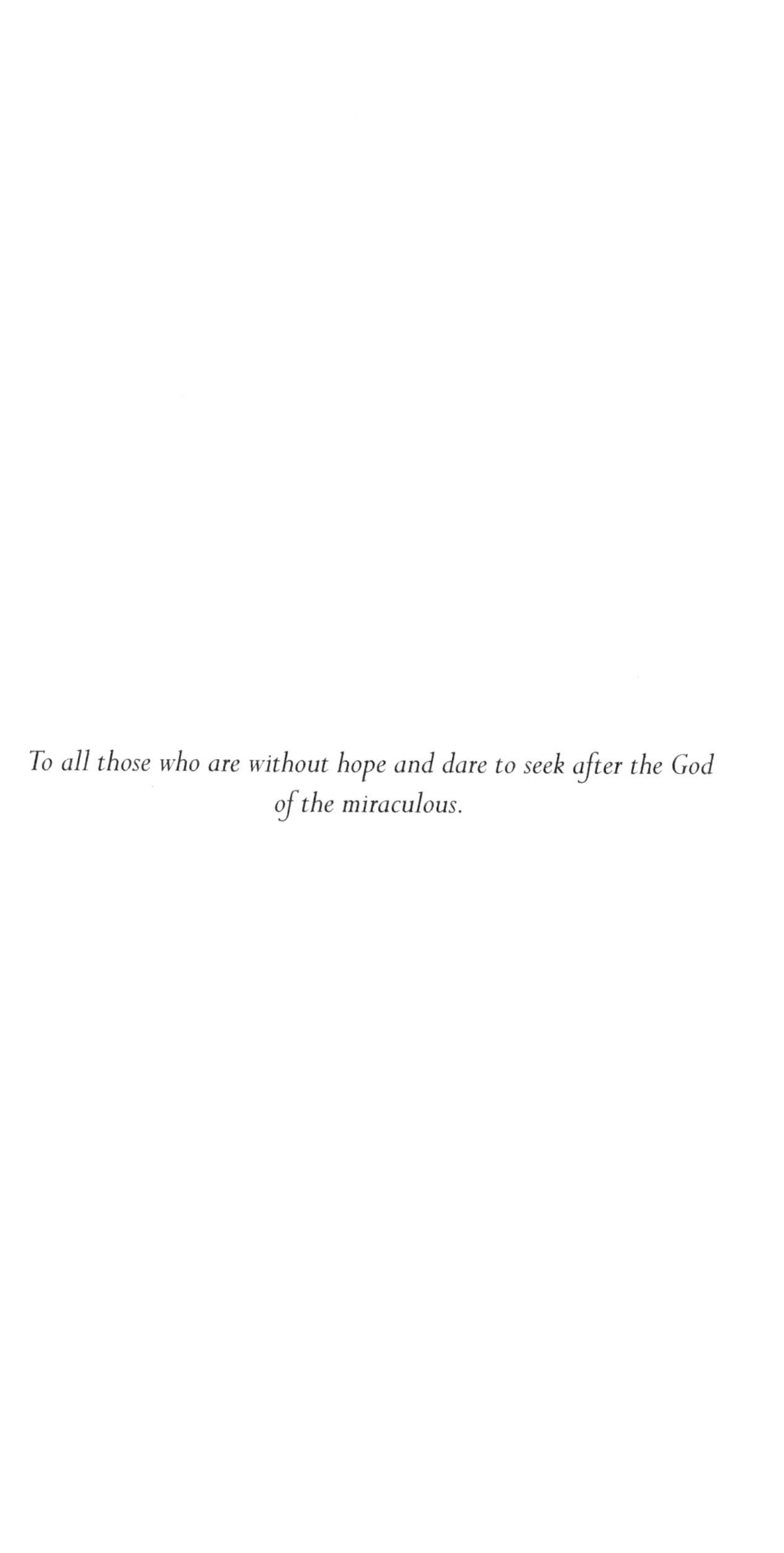

To all those who are without hope and dare to seek after the God of the miraculous.

Acknowledgments

We acknowledge all those who have helped us in this endeavor and all those who have given testimony to this miracle. We especially thank University Christian School for their permission to use the photographs illustrating that Dr. Ricky Roberts was in a special education class and was classified as mentally disabled at one time. We thank also those who helped in the proofreading of this manuscript.

Table of Contents

Foreword

By a Healed Dr. Ricky Roberts

This book chronicles the life, suffering and progress through many years of struggle against the attacks of Satan who battled to keep me enslaved to a diagnosis of mental retardation. My complete healing is the result of many tears and cries to Almighty God on my behalf that are found in the pages of this book.

The purpose of this book is not for my mother to recount the complete history of my life as a retarded person. Being a Ph.D., I could have easily written that book with a higher level of comprehension. I saw from the very beginning that the true purpose of this book was to focus on the miraculous background leading to the miracle itself, the cost of gaining such an amazing miracle from God and the miracle's aftermath. This book needed to be written by the one who cried bitterly for my healing more than all others, my mother. I am honoring her faith, her life and her struggle for my healing. If she had not stood in the gap for me,

I may never have been healed. Indeed, I may have even totally succumbed to the devices of Satan and his forces.

By looking at the outer person, we cannot realize the struggle and hurt that he or she has inwardly endured. My mother has suffered many combat wounds from fighting fiercely on my behalf. Instead of praising her battle for her retarded son, many people seem to envy my healing or feel jealous about the miracle that she gained. They do not realize that what God did through her can be done through all willing vessels. There is a great cost to be paid, however. My mother did not let the emotions, thoughts and ideas of others stop her from pushing forward to touch the hem of Jesus' garment. She was willing to pay the cost of stretching out to touch the Master's robe so that her retarded child could be healed from disability. What was the cost that she was willing to pay? She paid the cost of being an intercessor, putting God first above all else and giving Him everything.

I am able to write this foreword as a thankful servant of the Most High God who has been healed from retardation because my mother touched the heart of Almighty God. I can say nothing about my healing in any sense, except that it was an awesome act of grace. I am speechless and overwhelmed by the mercy of God in my life. Out of the approximately fifty students in University Christian's special education class over the years I attended, upon only one did God's grace fall in such a manner as to heal him of retardation. I am that person and my healing is for the glory of God alone!

This awesome act of love that saved me from a state of hopelessness is almost indescribable. I would not wish upon anyone the curse that I experienced as a mentally challenged individual—the laughter, jokes, funny looks, dislike and embarrassment that were the norm of my life.

As a person restored, I cry bitter tears over all those children and adults who have not been set free from their handicap. I seek God for their deliverance and pray that someone will touch the hem of His garment for them!

Ancient civilizations considered retardation (like seizures) an affliction from the gods. To me, the only word that can describe retardation in all its disguises is the word *curse*. I don't feel that being mentally challenged was a state of blessing for me; those who say that it is have never lived with it. If they could experience for one moment the effects of such an affliction, they would take back these sentiments. How can a life of retardation be a blessing? I do know that I would never want that "blessing" back! Since God healed me from that affliction over forty years ago, I have not missed a day of that adversity. I can now live in freedom, because of my deliverance by a mighty and merciful God.

A mental disability destroys all elements of time, space and dignity within a person's life. If God does not move to prevent it, all hope, promise and life can also be obliterated. There is no recollection of responsibility within a retarded person's life, leaving emptiness of mind and sometimes body. As a retarded person, I felt no glimmer of hope or promise without God.

It is this miserable state that has left many to believe the retarded are less than human. This evil philosophy, espoused by Nazi Germany, pushed for the killing of the retarded during World War II. It is also this outlook that helps promote the murdering of the unborn today through abortion.

Given the morals of today's society, perhaps I would have been aborted to rescue society from an unwanted burden. Think about it! If I had been aborted, I would never have suffered the horror of retardation. But God would have been robbed of a miracle. Retardation is not God's fault but our own! I don't attribute my retardation to God. Instead I point to the sin of man as its root cause.

As a disabled person, I lived in my own little world. In my early years, I did not worry about how my life would be as an adult. The retardation blinded me from realizing the hopelessness I would face as an adult if God did not heal me.

If it were possible for embarrassment to kill, it would have murdered me countless times. My whole life as a retarded child was filled with embarrassment. I was self-conscious about learning, living, walking, eating, talking, my weight, and my inability to read, have friends and express myself as God intended. In essence, the first sixteen years of my life can best be described as a Greek Tragedy: When hope would surface for a partially normal life, disappointment and disaster would raise their ugly heads and destroy it. No peace was there!

My life as a retarded person was such that I had to pay to have friends. I always felt alone, even in the midst of a crowd—an outcast, never fitting in anywhere—a broken vessel, thrown away by the world, through Satan's devices. In essence, I saw myself as the worst of the worst and the most miserable of the miserable. During all the time of my retardation, I can remember little happiness and no real life. I was physically breathing, yet there was no vitality to my emotions, thoughts or mind. My spirit was normal and cried out for healing from God even though my mind was traumatized by the state of retardation.

I can recall the many times in which I found myself pretending to read even though I could not recognize a single word. At the barbershop, I would pretend to read magazines even though the only things I really comprehended were the pictures. In the midst of my retardation, I became fearful of all books but the Bible. This seemed to be my Waterloo, where I would go down in total defeat. God, through His grace, changed what I thought was my downfall into my victory, by healing my retardation.

Since God has allowed me to retain the memories of my retardation, I can easily recall the times in which I was called "retarded," "stupid," "idiot" and "moron." Untold harm and hurt resulted from these words being spoken. I realize now that they were spoken out of ignorance and fear: Many people are uneasy about what is abnormal and often express it as hatred. Since my mind was affected rather than my spirit, the meaning of all these words was filtered through my spirit, and I sought after the God of the miraculous, crying out to Him for assistance. It was my spirit that said, "Forgive them, for they know not what they do!"

Even now, I must admit that some church people look at me as an outcast or somewhat strange. They seem unable to grasp the scope of the miraculous that touched my life. They are satisfied with living their lives, not realizing how much more that God could do if they allowed Him.

In some circles criticism against me is common, denouncing my higher education as useless. While I was working on my degree, a man prophesied that it was not God's will for me to study ancient languages and continue my college education. I am so thankful that I know His voice and His written Word! That prophecy was not in agreement with God's written Word.

How could I be able to go to college, study languages and receive advanced degrees? It was not because of my own ability and capacity! All of these things came because of the grace of God shining upon my life in a miraculous way.

As the reader will discover, the aftermath of such an awesome act of grace continues. I have been led in many ways as God has directed; not only was I led to go to college, but I was also directed to study ancient languages and theology. God then guided me to form a ministry. All of this came through someone who could not comprehend or understand any of these things by his own ability. God's miracle of grace is that He can take that which is considered useless and turn it into a miracle of His design and purpose.

In March of 1999, I founded a nondenominational ministry known as "True Light Ministries," based upon 1 John 2:8. Its purpose is defined as: "We follow the 'Old Way' already trodden down by the early church in its first three hundred years and follow their landmarks back to the cross and back to the original Christian faith. We seek to study the Word of God in the original languages and to understand what the early church taught."

Since the founding of this ministry, thousands confirmed healings, miracles and deliverances have taken place. More than hundreds of prophecies have been fulfilled. There have also been several other manifestations. Many have experienced countless signs of flowing oil upon walls, windows and foreheads of people. This fulfills Zechariah 4:14, and confirms the belief in the fresh oil which represents fresh anointing.

There was one manifestation of the oil that I will never forget. I had forgotten my own bottle of oil and had to borrow one with very little liquid in it. I said, "God will provide the oil we need." As I was teaching the Word of God, oil multiplied within the bottle and its color changed to a cloudy white. Everyone present saw this sign and wonder. I continued to teach God's Word. When I ended my instruction, I lifted up the bottle and took off the top. The most wonderful fragrance filled the church. Under the direction of the Lord, I tasted the oil. Its taste was that of a very expensive perfume. This manifestation took place in Alma, Georgia, in the year 2000, when I was thirty-eight years old and teaching on the last days. The oil was to be used to anoint people for prayer in accordance with James 5:13–18 and Mark 6:13.

I firmly believe that someone else was originally called to take on this ministry and to experience these manifestations of the Spirit. I also believe that this same person rejected his or her calling and election, causing God to look for one who would obey Him and do as He directed. As God looked upon a retarded teenager, He saw a hopeless life and a broken vessel that the world would never accept. God chose "the foolish things... to confound the wise" and the world (1 Corinthians 1:27).

He chose me, that broken instrument, having nothing to lose and everything to gain. I owe God my all: my ability, capacity, understanding, comprehension, mind, ministry, manifestations of the Spirit and health. I deserved none of these things then and do not deserve them now.

Soon after I was healed, the Lord Himself told me two very important things that have been burned into my consciousness. The first was, "Ricky, if you forget everything that I ever told you, forget not that the One who giveth can taketh away." The second one was, "Ricky, I will never, as long as you live, take away from you the memories of your retardation. They will remain in your mind as a memorial unto where I have brought you from."

I praise God that He healed a retarded teenager for His glory, His grace and the coming Great Awakening.

Over the many years since the last publication of this work, I have learned more deeply about how Satan works. (Doing exorcisms and other types of deliverances will tend to make you either swim or drown.) I regret that the knowledge I now have, I did not have in the past. If only my mother, my father, or I would have learned these truths back then, the fires may have been put out more easily. Through much warfare I have noticed that Satan follows certain types of repetitive patterns in families and in individual lives. In many respects, this book was written to identify the satanic patterns that destroy so many families. If you can uncover these patterns in your life, you will be able to combat Satan and his demonic forces with greater success and have the opportunity to win at the end.

VERBUM IPSE DEUS

Introduction

By a Healed Dr. Ricky Roberts

Long before the dawn of the Reformation, a holy saint of God made a powerful statement. His name was Tertullian and he was a leader of the church in the third century. His statement rocks the very foundation of modern theologies and all the theologies fashioned since the Reformation. In dealing with the apostate Marcion, who defected from the early church, Tertullian said:

> Atque ita constabit apostolus de quibus dixerit, de eis scilicet, quae futura erant in ecclesia eius dei, qui dum est, spiritus quoque eius operatur et promissio celebrator (And so, it will certainly be well known from what the Apostle has spoken, even of those things which were occurring in the church of His God; who as long as He lives, His Spirit also works, and His promises are repeated in great numbers).[1]

What force there is in Tertullian's argument!

Those who deny the continuation of the supernatural gifts so deny the continuation of God enduring and the Holy Spirit still working.

The history of the church is filled with the manifestations of the Holy Spirit. Remove those manifestations and church history is not only incomplete, but also lifeless. Christianity without these supernatural manifestations of the Holy Spirit is nothing more than a dead religion and a dead hope. Miracles are what distinguish Christianity from simple theism. History proves that these signs were not counterfeit as some people may imagine.

The early church and revivalists like John Wesley, all dogmatically taught that the supernatural gifts of the Holy Spirit and their outward manifestations had not yet ceased. When Reverend Middleton declared that the gifts and their manifestations had been withdrawn, Wesley cried out, "O Sir, mention this no more. I entreat you, never name their silence again. They speak loud enough to shame you as long as you live."[2]

In the Great Awakening, headed by Jonathan Edwards, there were many manifestations of the Holy Spirit. Some voiced such concern about these supernatural gifts and their manifestations that they accused the entire Great Awakening Movement of being in league with Satan. Jonathan Edwards refuted those accusations and preached on the genuine and counterfeit signs, affirming that what had occurred in the Great Awakening was genuine. Indeed, Jonathan Edwards concluded that God could still perform miracles, speak to His people, show dreams and visions and work all sorts of other manifestations.

In his writings, Edwards describes many persons who, in his day, were the subjects of the extraordinary work of the Holy

Spirit. He describes one person who continued for five or six hours in a vision of Christ. When the vision ended, the person thought that only a minute had passed. Extraordinary views of divine things such as prophecy, tongues and the like manifested themselves frequently in this revival. Some people for a time could neither stand nor speak. Others experienced their hands clenched and their flesh cold while their senses remained intact. Some shook uncontrollably and fell to the ground. An extraordinary sense of the awesome majesty, greatness and holiness of God overwhelmed the soul and body of all that witnessed these manifestations of the Spirit, and a sense of repentance filled the whole revival.

On the continuation of the supernatural gifts of the Holy Spirit and their manifestations, Edwards confesses, "The whole tenor of the Gospel proves it; all the notion of religion that the Scripture gives us confirms it."[3] In his work entitled *Mark of a Work of the True Spirit*, he says that the Holy Spirit, "has brought to pass new things, strange works, and has wrought enough to surprise both men and angels. As God has done thus in times past, so we have no reason to think but that He will do so still."[4]

Did not Paul himself say that the gospel of Christ was fulfilled in His ministry "through mighty signs and wonders, by the power of the Spirit of God" (Romans 15:19)? Without the manifestations of the Holy Spirit, the gospel cannot be fulfilled. No wonder the early church said that the gospel of the apostles was truly full and that the apostles and their disciples taught the "full gospel." The failure of the church at large today is due in great part to its rejection of the Holy Spirit, His gifts and the manifestations of these gifts in the church. The church has failed to give the Holy Spirit His rightful place.

This book is about the miracles of God still being alive and well. It is about the miraculous act of God when faith is not blinded or weakened but looks into the realm of the impossible for God's assistance. It is about believing that God's Spirit will work as long as He endures. It is about proclaiming to a child that God is still a God of the miraculous and telling him or her to reach out to that God. It is a witness that in the craziness of this world, God still performs miracles and healings. It is a proclamation to all the saints to retain their faith, no matter what happens. It is an exhortation to stand strong, no matter what opposition Satan puts one through. It is a vindication that, along with the angels, Our God liveth!

Miracles and healings of all sorts are the bread of the saints. (See Matthew 15:26.)They are indications that God is alive and well upon this planet and that the Word of God has been and continues to be sustained, substantiated and proven. These manifestations of the Spirit bring freedom since the Lord is there and working before the people. (See Isaiah 61:1.) Did not Paul himself say, "Where the Spirit of the Lord is, there is liberty" (2 Corinthians 3:17)? How does the Holy Spirit bring liberty? He brings it through His supernatural manifestations, whatever they may be.

The belief that God is still the God of the miraculous is our only hope when the storms of life are raging and times of suffering leave us gasping. This belief is often sparked by God's promise (whether from the Scriptures themselves or through a word given) that He will move and perform the miraculous in our lives. That belief becomes a pillar and a foundation that cannot be toppled by the pounding waters of Satan's oppression. We can stand like Daniel, still looking to the God of the miraculous, with an assurance beyond this realm that God will move and rescue us. We need to continue to hold on to Him by meeting, keeping and fulfilling His conditions, no matter what happens.

Our life was so ravaged by suffering that no peace or rest penetrated our lives. Many times as my mother would drive to work, she would cry out to God for death. The storms began before I was born and continued for over thirty years. Only now are we experiencing some peace and rest in our lives. St. Paul said that in order to reign with Christ, we must suffer. (See 2 Timothy 2:12.) My family and I are living witnesses to this scripture. Satan often tried to destroy the lives of my father, my mother and me. He sought to prevent God's intentions and purposes for our lives and might have succeeded if my father and mother had not held on to believing God above everything else.

It is important to remember that Paul saw the state of suffering and the state of grace joined as one whole. First Peter 5:10 reminds us that the victorious Christian can only be seen through the state of suffering. By yielding to this suffering, we will learn humility and reverence. (See Romans 12:12.)

It was during these times of great suffering that my mother cried many bitter tears over my life of retardation. It was at this time that God placed her tears into a bottle as a memorial of God's grace that would be poured out upon me. Remember David! David said, "Put thou my tears into thy bottle" (Psalm 56:8).

She learned the meaning of this expression while going through the pain. "O eyes, no eyes, but fountains fraught with tears! O Life, no life, but lively form of death!"[5] It was then that she knew "out of the presses of pain cometh the soul's best wine and the eyes, which shed no tears, can shed but little shine and glory!"[6]

I am convinced that her tears reached the very heart of God. These tears became the backbone of the ministry that was to come forth. Her tears nourished this ministry and gave birth to it. It was prophesied, "Every tear that she sowed in prayer was a seed which the Lord received that will bring forth a million-fold blessing and harvest that God will produce in the ministry!" Tertullian once said that the blood of the martyrs nourished the church. My ministry and life have been nourished in the same way by the tears of my mother. The Psalmist said, "They that sow in tears shall reap in joy. He that goeth forth and weepeth, bearing precious seed, shall doubtless come again with rejoicing, bringing his sheaves with him" (Psalm 126:5–6).

Tears, deep feeling and emotion are important parts of prayer. Emotional experiences often move us to pray. Many times tears are the visible sign that God is working in us. They seem to refresh the very working of our spirits. Tears can be seen as mirror images of our very beings. It can well be said that they contain our thoughts, feelings, memories, failures and successes.

Further, they also symbolize the surrendering of ourselves to God. (See Psalms 42:3; 56:8; 126:5; Acts 20:19; 2 Kings 20:5.)

When God speaks to us, we often anticipate Him working at warp speed to accomplish what He has promised. The problem is that God does not always work as fast as we want Him to work. Sometimes He delays to test our faith. When this happens, we must stand firmly, holding on when there is no hope. We need to be like the patriarchs and other saints of the

Old Testament who believed and held on whether they received their promise or not. (See Hebrews 11:1–13.)

A. W. Tozer once said, "The Bible was written in tears and to tears it will yield its best treasure."[7] The Bible may be said to be "a theology of tears." It was the tears of Hezekiah that touched God and moved God to heal him. (See 2 Kings 20:1.) Notice that Hezekiah mixed his prayers with tears and found acceptance. David said that his tears were his meat day and night. (See Psalm 42:3.)

God views tears as a sign of trust. They symbolize that we trust Him for our home, our lives and all our possessions. God sees tears as a glorious sign that we are surrendering to Him. They are the bursting forth of total surrender to a merciful God.

The ministries of the prophets and the apostles were founded upon their tears. Their weeping affected what they thundered in words. Their cries reached the throne of God and He granted them assistance and commissioned them for mission.

The early saints saw tears as a sign of repentance and a cleansing agent of the Lord. The tears of the woman who cried out for Jesus were a sign of her repentance and sorrow. (See Matthew 26:7–13.) These same believers beseeched the Lord in travail and repentance. They believed that lamentation and tears could touch the heart of God when nothing else could. These men and women understood that God saw Hezekiah's tears and was moved to extend his life. (See 2 Kings 20:1.) When two or more saints shed tears over a believer, Christ also sheds tears and prays for mercy. God is satisfied with faithful tears that are shed from eyes that have looked upon wickedness. Tears are sent forth as ambassadors to God to relay our sufferings.

The Jews believed that the tears of the Jewish women touched God so much that He caused Pharaoh to set the Jewish nation free. These tears turned God's face toward the Jewish people rather than turning it away because of their sin. The tears of the women touched God deeply.

My mother often said that she believed that she cried a river of tears stretching from Jacksonville to Fernandina, Florida. Her commuting time to work became her prayer time. While experiencing these bitter tears, my mother would wonder if God had forsaken us. She sometimes questioned God's presence with us. But He was always there, right in the midst of the storms, never forsaking or abandoning us. (See Hebrews 13:5.)

God's promises are utterly reliable and dependable. God cannot lie! He has never left us even if He sometimes seems far away. Deliverance will come, but it may take longer than we want. Redemption comes in God's timing, not our own. (See Ecclesiastes 3 and Psalm 34:19.) If we forget that and blame God for our failures, we bring destruction upon our lives.

Even David himself said in Psalm 22:1, "My God, my God, why hast thou forsaken me?" This verse teaches us that there are many times when suffering causes us to think that we are alone, without God and His love.

A nineteenth century poet, Frederick W. Faber, expressed so eloquently this seeming absence of God in times of trouble:

He hides Himself so wondrously
As though there were no God;
He is least seen when all the powers
of ill are most abroad.
Or He deserts us at the hour

The fight is almost lost.
And seems to leave us to ourselves
Just when we need Him most
It is not so, but so it looks;
And we lose courage then;
And doubts will come if God hath kept
His promise to men.[8]

Someone once said, "God is not the God over troubled waters but the God through troubled waters." It is God who carries us through the storms of life. He showers us with blessings and delivers us after the storms of life blow over. God will pull us through but we have to be able to withstand His grip. This pulling often can bring pain and anguish because we do not understand what God wants. But we can gain the victory over the turbulence if we learn to be more like Christ. The philosophy of the cross is, "We must decrease and He must increase."

Cry out to the God of the miraculous as our whole family did. Beseech Him to touch those who seem untouchable or appear to have no hope. God is the God of the hopeless as is evidenced by my life. Without Him, there was no hope for me. Our family motto became: "We would rather believe and not receive than could have believed and could have received." We held on by not giving in, not giving up and not giving out. The promises that God made in His Word regarding healing and miracles became our victory cry. We had simple and uneducated faith that these promises were valid and we did whatever God demanded of us. What God desires most is that we reach up to Him so that He can reach down to us!

CHAPTER 1

Beginnings of a Miracle

My husband, George Elias Roberts, and I were raised just twenty miles apart from each other. Both our fathers worked as farmers during the Great Depression.

My husband was born prematurely and was not supposed to live. There was little in the way of hospital care, money or proper equipment to handle a baby born so early. He was so small that the family related that "his bed was a shoe box." His sister remembers that his mother's wedding ring could slide up his arm to the elbow. Because of this premature birth, he had to be watched twenty-four hours a day, kept at a very warm temperature and fed with an eye-dropper. These circumstances were difficult because the house that the family lived in was old, cold and drafty with many holes in the walls and a sole fireplace as the only heat.

Since almost everyone around Coffee County, Georgia, had lost their possessions during the Great Depression, a family was fortunate to have food on the table and a place to live. A doctor was positively a luxury. Any town lucky enough to have a doctor usually paid him with bacon, ham or chickens. Since these were very dear, most of the poor families used old medicinal remedies to treat illness instead.

The circumstances of those difficult times were no different for Elias, though it helped that his grandmother Lanie was a midwife. In the course of her work she had seen so many premature babies die and knew that her grandson would need a miracle to survive. In addition to being a prayer warrior, Grandmother Lanie was also a jack-of-all-trades. She was a midwife, intercessor, and a retailer selling eggs and other things grown on the farm. She could do a little preaching, too! She was the one who taught my mother-in-law how to pray.

Many godly men and women living in the Great Depression found time to pray all night. They also made it a point to fast during these hard times. Though many had lost most of their worldly possessions, their faith and time with God never lessened. In fact, the hard times made them stronger in their faith even while others were undergoing financial and spiritual collapse all around. Many became shipwrecked in their faith while others, by the grace of God, found their faith. These people persevered in their faith by never giving in, never giving up and never giving out.

Elias was very sickly for most of his life. He described having the worst "swimming headaches" as a young child. These types of headaches are similar to migraines but with some medical differences. Elias often talked about carrying water in a bucket to his father in the field and having these headaches begin. When this took place, he would actually see the field turning around and would often vomit. He was unable to hold up his head and would have to be carried back to the house.

Thank God for praying saints! The family had a neighbor known as "Jumping Jim Carter" who had an ice route. One day Jim Carter found Elias sick with one of his headaches when he came to deliver ice. Mrs. Roberts asked Brother Carter if he had time to pray for Elias. His answer was, "I always have time to pray for someone who's sick." After Brother Carter prayed for Elias, his swimming headaches completely disappeared.

God's infinite mercy touched Elias and delivered him from those horrible headaches through Brother Carter's prayer. Fifty years later God allowed Elias to be instrumental in laying the foundation for Brother Carter's great-great-grandson to be saved.

So often Satan tried his best to see that Elias was killed or injured. When he was seven or eight years old, his oldest brother, J. H., carried him down to a water hole to go swimming. Elias jumped in and landed on a log underneath the water, causing severe damage and pain to his lower back. The damage and pain were so bad that J. H. thought that Elias was dead and had broken his back. It took some time before Elias could walk again. The pain never left him even though God healed him of many illnesses and injuries after that. Yet, Elias never allowed this pain to get the better of him. Many days he worked tirelessly despite the pain to provide for our family.

As Charles Dickens once said, "It was the best of times; it was the worst of times." Our parents did not think that education was important. They taught us how to work and thought that was the only education that we needed. Dealing with this attitude of prejudice against education forced Elias to remain uneducated, keeping him tied to farm work as a means to make a living. Although his formal education extended only through the third grade, he had a head full of common sense. However, Satan deprived him of the opportunity to study and be well rounded. We will never know what might have happened if people then had been more versed in spiritual warfare. Maybe more would have opposed Satan's plans and devices.

Remember what Jesus said about Satan and later about Himself? "The thief cometh not, but for to steal, and to kill, and to destroy: I am come that they might have life, and that they might have it more abundantly" (John 10:10). Notice that Christ says here that the saints can have life more abundantly. In Elias' early life, Satan stole many things from him due to a lack of knowledge rather than the presence of sin. No one in that area was teaching the Word of God as it should be taught. Friends and family were unable to attend church regularly so that they could learn the means to fight Satan. Going to church involved either a mule-drawn wagon or a late night walk through the woods. Their concern was not so much about how to fight Satan as it was how to survive.

The Word of God says, "My people are destroyed for lack of knowledge: because thou hast rejected knowledge, I will also reject thee, that thou shalt be no priest to me: seeing thou hast forgotten the law of thy God, I will also forget thy children" (Hosea 4:6). The rejection of knowledge, especially godly knowledge, destroys people. Wisdom, and a well-rounded education that is grounded upon the Word of God, will bring life and deliverance.

Satan repeatedly wins by deception and ignorance. Paul himself said, "Lest Satan should get an advantage of us: for we are not ignorant of his devices" (2 Corinthians 2:11). We can learn how Satan operates through our study of the Scriptures, the Holy Spirit and our experience. We must not be ignorant of Satan and his devices. When we're uninformed, we reap nothing but evil and destruction. We need to realize that as soon as one battle ends, another begins. The Christian walk is filled with battles ending and battles beginning, because Satan never gives up fighting against a saint.

Despite the limitation of his environment, Elias was able to hold down jobs. In fact, he worked for forty-one years operating a machine that makes cardboard boxes for two different companies. God gave him the ability to listen to the corrugator machine running and, just by listening, to diagnose what was wrong with it. For this talent he was named, "Mister Corrugator of America." He was offered a job with a large company that involved traveling about the country, installing corrugators and teaching others how to use this very large machine. Because he knew that I could not raise our retarded son Ricky alone, he had to turn down this wonderful job opportunity. Yet, he did not regret rejecting this offer. His son and our family were more important to him than anything in the world. From the time that Ricky was born until he was six years old, he slept in our bed under Elias' arm. If Ricky had a convulsion while we were sleeping, Elias would know immediately what was wrong. He would often wake me up to get a spoon to put on Ricky's tongue. If this happened we knew that we were on the way to the hospital again.

Elias was the kind of man who was unselfish, putting his child before everything but his relationship with the Lord. He was always willing to get up and cook something for Ricky to eat if he became hungry during the night. Because of Ricky's sickly disposition, whenever he wanted something to eat, we gave it to him. To us, Ricky's hunger was a sign that he was all right.

Elias was never too tired to carry Ricky to kindergarten or to a tutor. He also was willing to cook, wash and take care of Ricky for me when I had to work. He was familiar with the working of the house and relieved me of much responsibility. Some of the best times that I remember were when we cooked, gardened and canned fresh vegetables together. He had helped his mother in the same way when he was younger. His mother often said that he would never leave her side while she was still canning. He would stay with her no matter the day, the hour or the circumstance. The kitchen would have to be cleaned completely so that when he sat down, she could sit down too.

If there is such a thing as a godly seed, I believe that it was placed in Elias from the beginning because he was always a family man. He loved his home and family. His mother said that Elias never gave her any trouble. He was kind and gentle. The only time that she could remember him getting in trouble was in his early years. Before he was saved he decided to drink moonshine and got very drunk. He tried to slip up the steps to his room without her knowing it. But she noticed that he did not wash his feet. Every night, even as a young child, he took a bath and then washed his feet before going to sleep. Yet, this night he did not take a bath or wash his feet but slipped up to bed. When she came into his room and found out that he was drunk, she woke him up and had a long talk with him. This conversation alone was enough to make him never want to drink again. God was preparing him for the life that was before him.

Elias was a man who truly loved all children, especially his own. When we would go to Georgia on a visit, we would take the nephews and nieces fishing and hunting. If the nephews wanted the catch cooked at three or four o'clock in the morning, he would clean and cook it for them. When they all went hunting, he taught them the right way to use a shotgun. At my husband's funeral, one nephew said that Elias could have had fifty children and enjoyed every one of them.

Elias had four brothers and one sister. When his oldest brother brought Elias to my house when I was eight years old, Elias said, "I will marry that girl, Dot." He always remembered how I was dressed that day, in a blue shirt and overalls with my hair cut short. I must have made an impression on him even though he was three years older! He did not make the same impact on me because I just do not remember him at that age. Later on he got my attention so completely that I married him.

From afar, he watched me grow up. I had a blind date with him when I was older. I was in Douglas, Georgia, one Saturday when my girlfriend came up and asked whether I would go out with her and her boyfriend, who was a cousin of Elias. Knowing that the purpose was that I would date Elias, I at first said no because I didn't date anyone I didn't know. Yet, I changed my mind. We went to a theater that night and dated a few times later. After several dates he assumed that we were going steady even though I knew nothing about it. Then suddenly he left town.

When he came back, I was not the same young woman that he left. During his absence I had met Jesus. From that time on I only dated boys who attended the Church of God. Elias had no problem with that. In fact, we became hard workers for the Lord together. We would pick up young people and carry them to church with us. Our local preacher was so impressed that he preached a sermon called "Working for the Lord" and dedicated it to both of us.

We both had a heart for our families and wanted God to use us to touch them as well. Though our fathers had similar professions, their lives were very different. My father had been married to a cherished lady named Lillie before my mother ever knew him. They had one daughter and were expecting their second child when tragedy struck. A man just released from prison murdered Lillie and her unborn child. My father and another friend had used their influence to have this man released from the chain gang. Within ten days of his release, he committed this horrific murder while my father and a farmworker were working in the field. The brutality of this murder shocked the whole community and was unheard of at this time in Georgia.

The fiendishness of the murder was so great that it disturbed and shook the whole nation. It was reported in the Associated Press and national newspapers on May 2, 1918. The Cordelle Dispatch reported on the murder, recording:

> *Mrs. Simmons was a small woman, but she was not frail. If there was the slightest resistance to the brute attack, there was no evidence left. The dining room, stove, and a table containing the*

cooking things in the small cook room were in their place and not disordered. If anything was thrown to the floor in a scuffle, it had been replaced by the fiend. Only two bloody table forks were found in the yard. The bludgeon with which Mrs. Simmons head was battered to a pulp with was nowhere to be found.... Further, Mrs. Simmons was attacked with forks. She was stabbed so often with the fork attack that the top of a pepper duster could not have possibly contained more perforations. The forks were both bent up in the attack so as to render them useless in a further assault of this character. This stabbing with the forks indicated that the murderer thought thus to reach her heart and end her life. But the bludgeon was apparently later used and as many as five or six terrible strokes were plainly apparent in the different apertures in her head on the right side in the temple and over the right eye. Her sewing was still under the needle of her machine on the front porch of the house. Her shoes were in the room adjoining the kitchen. She lay in her stocking feet, her dress and underwear partially stripped away from her neck and right shoulder, but still pinned with two safety pins. About her throat were slight signs that she may have first been choked into insensibility, and around her, the blood from her body had flowed directly across the room. Her brains were shattered and scattered to the walls of the kitchen by the powerful strokes of the implement of death used by the brute....[1]

The shock of the horrifying experience of finding his wife murdered and seeing his first child crawling in the blood of her dead mother left unimaginable scars on my father that just could not be healed without divine intervention. It is the baptism of the

Holy Spirit and spiritual gifts that release the power of God to set people free. Remember that Psalm 55:22 says, "Cast thy burden upon the LORD, and he shall sustain thee: he shall never suffer the righteous to be moved."

The problem, however, was that my father was not saved! If he had been saved, this horrifying tragedy might never have taken place. If only he had walked in the arms of Jesus all his life, this murder might not have seen the light of day. If he had known Jesus he would not have had to carry this burden until he was seventy-five years old and finally saved. If he had only confessed with his mouth the Lord Jesus and believed with his heart, he would have received divine help.

After the murder and before my father married his second wife, who became my mother, something strange and demonic took place in his life. It began very simply. He had a new horse and buggy and was traveling by a cemetery near dusk. As he approached the cemetery, he stopped to step out of the buggy and began to walk the horse for a time. While he had stopped to give his horses a rest many times before, he never stopped by a cemetery. He had been raised to fear demonic activity, instead of believing in the protection of the blood of Christ. Because of his fear, he did not go near a cemetery since it was commonly believed that demons resided there.

Everything seemed all right at the cemetery until my father saw something gray that resembled a small dog such as a poodle. There were no dogs like this where my father lived in Georgia. Instead of fleeing the cemetery and this phenomenon of the supernatural, he ran after it and tried to pick it up. I do not know how long my father continued trying to grasp this apparition. I do know that it disappeared and he could not find it again. I believe that this apparition was a demonic spirit resembling the form of a dog because after this event, my father was never the same. It was as if something had possessed him that was not holy, good or righteous. I believe that he became demon-possessed.

Why would this apparition entice my father to follow it? I believe it was for his destruction! The Scriptures warn all humanity about trafficking with demonic spirits. (See Leviticus 20:6; Deuteronomy 18:11; 1 Samuel 28:7–25; 2 Kings 21:6; 23:24; 1 Chronicles 10:13; 2 Chronicles 33:6; Isaiah 8:19; 19:3; 29:4.) My father did this in ignorance, but others do it intentionally.

My mother came into the picture about three years later. When she married my father she got a ready-made family. Not once can I remember my mother complaining about her mother-in-law or about her stepchild. It seems, from all evidence, that she loved her stepdaughter as her own. His family and the family of his first wife were always welcomed in our house. My step-grandfather was often seen around our farm. There was no contention between the families, with all trying their best to get along and make what living they could.

My mother was strong, well rounded, well meaning, determined, hardworking and loved being at home. If she had not been, the marriage would have failed. In later years, my mother became so attached to her old home place that when my father built her a new house, her children had to go and move her out. She did not want to go, but agreed to it for the sake of her children. She centered her life around her family and her home.

There were six girls and just one boy in my family. Before World War II, and especially through the Great Depression, my father worked outside the farm and my mother hired men to help her work on the farm. It was often said that my father would work all day selling groceries, catch a train home at midnight or one A.M., and then walk about five miles with a sack filled with groceries that contained nothing but essentials. These were things that could not be grown on the farm such as salt, flour and coffee.

I am sorry to say that by the time I was born, the damaging effects of my father's past life had already taken a heavy toll on what remained of his life. He led a life of rebellion, drunkenness and debauchery. These ungodly manifestations were foreign to his upbringing and how he had lived before the tragedy hit his life. Before this time, my father had been a well-known baseball player. My father-in-law remarked that he had seen my father pitch in baseball games many times. Even though he worked in some capacity with the federal government, he still continued to work on his own farm.

He began drinking when he left the federal government and began working for the state government of Georgia. At that time he never drank anything stronger than soda. What put him on this path of destruction can be blamed in part on his participation in cocktail parties after closing. Drinking socially led him into deeper depths of sin. I believe that if he had any idea that this could have robbed him of his dignity and hurt his family, he would have never started down this path. Too many saints follow this slippery path back into sin and depravity. Paul himself warns in 1 Corinthians 6:9–10 and 1 Corinthians 9:27, that sin is death. "For the wages of sin is death; but the gift of God is eternal life through Jesus Christ our Lord" (Romans 6:23). My father truly tasted the wages of sin! Yet five years before he died, he tasted the divine presence of the Lord and the loving grace of God when he received the gift of eternal life. The salvation of a soul is what counts more than anything else. Thank God my father woke up before it was too late!

By the time I was six, my mother was leading three of her children into the field to plow, plant and break up the hard ground. Our lives depended on it. The farm sustained us in the worst of times. Because my mother excelled at both cooking and farming, she could teach anyone how to work on a farm. Countless times I watched her pick cotton so fast that it would bewilder the mind. It was said that she and the children could pick a full bale of cotton in two days. During this time, my alcoholic father was very little help.

Mother's cooking was legendary. Community lore said that if anyone tasted her cooking, they would never forget it. She never had any idea how many would eat at our table on a given day. People would feel her warm welcome even when they had invited themselves. After working for some time in the field, Mother would leave to go into the kitchen and begin to cook lunch or dinner. When the children came in to eat, there would always be plenty of food. At special times there would even be a churn of ice cream or old-fashioned teacakes. We worked hard and also ate very well. I often remember my mother going into a cold kitchen and cooking a large breakfast with homemade biscuits, homemade butter and homemade syrup. Despite having so many wonderful memories of my mother, I would never want those days to come back!

In later years, my mother's health began to fail and that put more work on all the children, especially after my sister married. When we came home from school, it was common for us to pick a wagonload of cucumbers to take to the market. We would take the wagon down by the railroad track at night and hope that no train would come by to frighten the mule. This would make him spill the cucumbers that we wanted to sell. We had to try to keep the mule calm so that we could keep all our cucumbers. These trips to the market gave my father extra money.

Though times were hard and money not easy to come by, we were always allowed to buy what we wanted to eat when we took our goods to market. Most of the time we bought an RC Cola and cinnamon buns, charging them to my father's account. My father didn't care what we bought as long as we did not waste the money or buy things he disapproved of. We knew what to buy and what not to buy. If we bought something that my father disapproved of, we knew that we would be punished. We did have to work for the money to buy our own clothes for school and for anything else.

All of us knew what it was to dip turpentine, cut trees down for wood, sit up all night to fire a tobacco barn and crop the tobacco the next morning. There were always mules to be fed and cows to be attended to. There was never time for rest, for prayer or for God. My father was wonderful when he was not drinking and would help anyone who was less fortunate. Yet when he drank, a force would take over his life and personality. He beat us so brutally that blood would sometimes flow from our backs. He never knew when to stop. It was quite easy for him to quote, "Spare not the rod." (See Proverbs 22:15; 23:13; 29:15.)

The last time I remember my father whipping me with a tobacco stick was when he was drinking. I received this beating because I could not plow a watermelon patch planted in a dried up and rocky field. It had not rained for a considerable length of time. When he whipped me on this occasion, I refused to cry. This made him very angry and he continued to hit me harder. My mother walked outside and saw what was going on. She ran to him, took away the tobacco stick and shouted, "You are going to kill her!" Finally he stopped. I was a young teenager at that time and warned him that it was the last time that he would beat me or ever lay his hands on me again. The next day he was very sorrowful over the whole incident, especially since he himself could not plow the same piece of field.

So often I remember my father leaving the house to go to town. I would wonder whether he was going to come back home drunk or sober. Due to his drunkenness and the horrible beatings the other children and I suffered, I often prayed to God as a child that my father would die before he came home. I prayed this as an innocent little child, not yet saved by the blood of Christ. Later, I thanked God that He knew best and did not grant my petition!

We were not a religious family, but occasionally went to church. Having no car, we had to walk. Despite our limited attendance, I saw evidence of my mother's faith frequently. She prayed and believed that it would rain before it was too late to save the crops. The rains would then come just in time. She always held to this faith and was never disappointed. Even my father was never too drunk to pray grace over his meal.

In these early years, God did not abandon my family or me. On one cold day when I was about five years of age, my overalls caught fire, and my leg was burned so badly that my parents thought I would never walk again. But a preacher was running a revival close to our house and was blessed with the power of the Holy Spirit upon his life. He came into my house and prayed for my leg. In a few days I was up and walking. God completely healed my leg.

I remember one Easter when my brother and I were walking to church. The Sunday school teacher at the church happened to be a lady who helped us put in tobacco. The next time we worked together she remarked that if everyone came to church all the time rather than just on Easter or Christmas, the church would be filled. I challenged her saying that even though she was my Sunday school teacher, there did not seem to be a difference between us. She smoked and cursed like I did. She smoked publicly while I snuck around so that my parents would not know. This conversation led my teacher to judge herself and accept the Lord as her Savior. I saw such a difference in her after that. In fact, she seemed very peculiar to me. The Scriptures say that the saints of God are "a peculiar people" (1 Peter 2:9). Notice that she was teaching the Word of God before she was saved. How many are either teaching or preaching the Word of God and are not saved today? Many people going to hell are those who are present at church and have never yet known that glorious relationship with Christ.

In a particular Church of God, there was a lady with whom my father had a sexual affair. This took place a long time before she was saved and a long time before she attended this church. I knew about the affair and was hurt over it. I did not like that particular Church of God because she attended it. The affair caused untold troubles in our family, especially to my mother.

Knowing this woman, I often swore that when I was grown, I would beat her senseless. I always remarked that if that church allowed women like this to go there, I did not want any part of that church. I did not realize that long after that affair had ended, the Lord Jesus had saved her, and she had become a new creation in Christ Jesus. There is a difference between the old you and the new you when Christ comes into your life. If not, there is no true conversion at all.

Another strike against this church was that it was Pentecostal. I was not familiar with it and had never seen what went on there. I had never experienced the shouting, the strange utterances of tongues, the healings, the miracles and the other manifestations of the Holy Spirit. The very first time I was exposed to these was a shocking experience. As it happened, I spent one night with my Aunt Hazel and my cousin. As the youngest teenager I had to sleep between them in the only bedroom. About four o'clock in the morning, I was awakened by the strange and awful commotion of my aunt jumping, shouting and speaking something strange which I had never heard in my life. I believe that my hair actually stood up. I ran behind my cousin and said, "If she gets me, she has to get you first!" When Aunt Hazel began to calm down, she lifted her hands in the air, walked into the kitchen, and all that I could hear her say was something like, "I thank the Ghost." From childhood, my family and I would sit around the fire and, on occasion, tell ghost stories. I was scared and ready to leave that place, even if I had to make a door to get out. When she walked back into the bedroom, I heard her plainly thanking the "Holy Ghost" and praising God for His visitation. As she was thanking the Lord, I was looking around to see if I could see the Lord, too. Finally, the manifestation of the Holy Spirit subsided. My aunt said, "Kids, we can go back to bed now." I pointed my finger at my cousin and said, "This time, you sleep beside her!" Often I heard my aunt say that she wanted to leave this world shouting and speaking in tongues. God granted her desire and that is just what happened.

One night as I was attending that same Church of God, a lady preacher, Sister Mae Terry, was the guest speaker. Her sermon was not a sermon made for itching ears, nor was it a sermon filled only with empty words. (See 2 Timothy 4:3.) Her words were ones of power.

In these later years, it reminds me of a sermon preached by Jonathan Edwards. The sermon was called "Sinners in the Hands of an Angry God." When Jonathan Edwards preached this sermon, the hearers felt hell and its torments all around them. So much conviction was wrought by this sermon that hundreds would run to the altar to be saved. Jonathan Edwards would continue to preach this sermon to new hearers. During Edwards' life, the sermon never became old or outdated because it had the fire of God within it.

Just like the sermon that Jonathan Edwards preached so long ago, Sister Mae Terry preached a hell, fire and brimstone sermon. I personally believed that the seat I was sitting on was on fire when she gave the altar call. At first, all I remember was that somehow I found myself down at the altar crying out to Jesus to save my soul. The next thing I remember was a woman behind me praying with her hand upon my back. Her hand felt like a warm iron. I turned around to see just who she was and saw the woman who had the affair with my father. That night God burned away all the bitterness and hatred that I had held for years against her. I truly became that new creation in Christ Jesus that Paul speaks of in 2 Corinthians 5:17. All the baggage of my life was unpacked and put away.

As a young teenager that night, I met and fell in love with Jesus. His love was a love that I knew nothing about. Once I experienced it, I was not going to give it up, whatever the cost. As if there were not enough tears already shed, there would be much more crying in the coming years for my son and for my family. I had no idea just how much I was going to need Jesus. I could neither imagine the pain or the anguish that I would endure.

When I was saved that night, the Church of God did not take it too seriously. They saw the type of family I was born into and concluded that I would never make it. But God knew that, "He which hath begun a good work in you will perform it until the day of Jesus Christ" (Philippians 1:6). That has been proven in my life! My salvation only provided greater reinforcement to my desire to remain sexually pure until marriage. I also decided to date boys who had found the same Savior that I had.

When I was saved that night, I began a life of intercessory prayer for my family. At this time, no one in my family was saved. I was the baby girl and the only one standing in the gap for my family. Next to be saved were my older sister and brother-in-law. For years the life and practice of intercessory prayer for my family (and especially for my father) did not bear much fruit that I could see. In fact, circumstances of life became worse. My father began to drink more instead of less. When I began to intercede for my family, I entered into the battle for their very souls. It did not seem as if I was gaining much ground for a time. All I could do was trust that the Lord would lead me every step of the way. I really did not even know how to pray. I would find a place in the field and cry out to God, learning how to pray in stages. I would pray on the school bus, walking, and even in my bed, crying until I went to sleep.

One particular Sunday I was in great travail over my family. After praying at the altar, I went to my Sunday school class to continue to pray. I felt such a heavy burden for my family that needed to be lifted. As I cried out to God for help, the Lord gave me a vision and told me that if I would serve Him, He would save my whole family, including my father. When the vision faded, I looked and saw my Aunt Hazel praying with me. At the time I had no idea that it would be twenty years before this vision would come true. God simply told me that my father would be saved. God gave me a piece of the puzzle, not all of the pieces at once. It might have seemed easier for God to give it all to me at once. But where would my faith have been?

During these twenty years my father's condition did not get any better but actually became worse. Later there would only be a few days that he would not be drinking. But even these days were terrible because he would suffer withdrawal symptoms. During these times it was very common for him to have hallucinations of elephants, pink rats running up the wall and other images. My mother finally gave up and put him in a hospital where he could receive help for his alcoholism. He was not ready to receive the help and became angrier than ever. When he finally left the hospital, he went back to the same type of life that he had before.

After this failed treatment I had to take my parents to the tobacco market one Saturday. I could tell that my father had been drinking that morning just like he did most days. I did not let on that I knew he had been drinking whiskey. I asked, "Dad, you have been good today. I know that you want a drink. Where do you buy your whiskey? It is time that this family acknowledges that we have an alcoholic father rather than being ashamed of it anymore." I gave him twenty dollars and took him to the liquor store. When he came out I said to him, "Is that enough to last till Monday?" I did not want him driving on the road in a drunken state. His remark to me was, "Now, let's not overdo this thing!" I said to him, "We have tried to get help for you to quit drinking with no success. The god that you serve is the god of alcoholism. When you die, I am going to put a fifth of whiskey in your coffin, because that fifth of whiskey is the god that is sending you to hell for all eternity!" My father was ready to receive help the following Monday morning. This time the hospital made it hard on him. The medical staff put him in with mental patients that had severe problems. My father was frightened for his very life. He prayed that if God would let him live, he would serve Him and never drink again. At that moment, my father was saved. His last testimony before his death was, "Since I have found the Master, I have found no detour signs." This same message was preached at my father's funeral.

Even though my father was saved, God was not finished with our family and had not yet fulfilled His entire promise to me. One by one, my family began to come into the fullness of the Lord. I have found that God always brings to pass what He promises, as long as we do our part. The last unsaved person in my family came to know the Lord only two years before the writing of this book.

CHAPTER 2

Battle for a Miracle

The spiritual warfare for my family began long before the battle for my son. The fight to receive a miracle for my son really began before I was married. The Lord was preparing me and warning me that there would be an assault ahead.

Elias and I prayed earnestly for a year about the decision to marry. In 1951, we tied the knot and soon afterward moved down to Jacksonville, Florida. We made this unheard of move away from everything that we knew, even though we had no money and a small job that paid very little. Unaware that God was moving us out of our safety zone, we found ourselves in Jacksonville in miserable conditions. For two years we barely survived. Cabbage and grits became our mainstay because they were cheap. It is amazing to me that even now I still enjoy eating them. After God saw that He could trust us with the little we had, He gave us better jobs and helped us save some money.

Before that, I relentlessly prayed that God would give me a good job even though it did not seem likely. I told Him that I would never use it selfishly. Elias and I continued to attend church even though we were looked down upon because we had such poor clothes. Elias even walked to work to save gas so that we could go to church. One night we decided to go to a church near our home. The preacher saw that I had no stockings on and preached against me not wearing them.

Easter was coming up and I realized that I would have to wear the same old dress that I had been wearing during the week. Finally, the Lord blessed me with a very good job. I began to put money back, dollar by dollar, to buy an expensive Easter outfit. I was able to save one hundred and fifty dollars, a huge sum to me at the time.

I had planned my shopping trip for the Saturday before Easter. I was so excited about getting a new dress! The Lord, however, had not forgotten my promise to Him that I would be unselfish with my earnings once I got my new job. The Wednesday before Easter, the Lord led me to a particular home. There I found an elderly woman and her disabled son. They were both very sick and had been to the doctor. They had no money to buy medicine or food. Their kitchen cabinets were bare and they had no gas to cook with.

I took their prescriptions to a pharmacy and ran into the grocery store. I decided to spend enough money to buy a little food for them, so that they could survive for a few days. As I was walking down the aisles, I will never forget what the Lord said to me.

The simple words I heard were, "Feed them as you want Me to feed you." I pushed down hard on the brakes of that cart. I decided to buy for them more than I would have bought for myself. When I checked out, I had spent all of the money that I had saved. I rose Easter Sunday and got ready to go to church.

Since I had spent my money, I had to wear a dress that was made of a heavy material and not really suitable for the Easter season. Evangelist T. L. Lowery was having a baptismal service in a tent. When I arrived, I decided to sit in the very back, hoping that no one would see me. But the Lord had other plans in mind! Our pastor and his wife had saved seats for us right down front.

As I sat down, I felt led to pray that I would be able to shout for joy, just as my Aunt Hazel once did.

The baptismal service seemed dead. In an instant of time though, the Holy Spirit began to move in our midst in a mighty way. All at once, I jumped up, ran down the aisle across the platform, and jumped into the baptismal pool shouting from one end to the other. The ushers could not pull me out of the pool. Our pastor said, "If that water is holy enough to make Dot Roberts shout, let us all go into it." There were several hundred baptized that day. I was the first one in and the last one out. My heavy dress went right into the water with me and did not come up over my head. God's plan was working all along.

In the tenth year of a childless marriage, the Lord led me to begin praying for a child. I remembered the prayers of the childless in the Bible and how God answered them. God put a seed of faith in my heart that led me to pray not just for a child, but also for a son. After praying for some time, the Lord told me to name my boy Ricky Elias Roberts. When my husband came home from work that night, I told him that we would have a son and what we were to name him. My husband was upset because he knew that my doctors had advised me not to have children due to medical reasons. I told him, "We are going to have faith to believe that God can bring me through this, or we can just hang up on this thing called faith. We are either going to believe or reject God's promise." I was fired-up and meant business. I was determined to push forward to receive what God had for me. Often we don't receive the things that God has for us because we won't push forward.

Nine months later our son was born. Even before the birth, our peace and rest disappeared. The pregnancy was not easy and I began to have all kinds of complications. Everything imaginable that could happen did happen in our lives. Satan literally came upon us like a flood. Satan is such a coward because he catches us at our weakest times and then turns all his forces loose against us.

Even in the midst of all the tribulation, God would use us to pray for people who were sick, and they would recover. This was especially true after my son was born. I felt as if I was experiencing the full gospel of the apostolic church. I saw God performing miracles and healings before my very eyes. I saw the words of Christ being fulfilled right in front of me, "They shall lay hands on the sick, and they shall recover" (Mark 16:18). I remembered the words of James also coming to pass, "And the prayer of faith shall save the sick, and the Lord shall raise him up; and if he have committed sins, they shall be forgiven him" (James 5:15).

During this time, Satan often put someone who was either fanatical or demon-possessed in my path. I remember meeting a recently saved woman who fanatically prophesied many crazy things. I began to fast up to twelve days at a time because I did not know how to handle this woman's situation and hysteria, nor did I know how to handle the spirit of deception that had fallen upon her. She actually believed that she was the reincarnation of a famous prophet. Finally, she prophesied that if Elias and her husband would go to a certain place, they would find a man that would be able to help her. There was no such man because he did not exist! She came to the realization that her prophecies were not of God and that she had been deceived. She repented of her sins and became spiritually balanced by following 1 John 5:5–10.

All of these experiences burdened me so much that I backed off from God and stayed in my safety zone for some time. In this lukewarm state, I found out that Satan left me alone because I was not challenging him. I found out that staying in the safety zone just doesn't work. Just as the mother eagle pushes her babies out of the nest, so the saint of God will have battles to go through to gain God's promise. As long as I remained in my comfort zone, Satan was winning the battle for my son because I was no threat to him. God challenged me to leave that place of security and I accepted. I was now ready to do battle for my family and son. I was ready to do spiritual warfare. I was ready to go through dark places. I was ready to seek after God and His presence more completely than I had ever done before. Whatever I had to fight, whatever battle I had to go through, I was ready. I decided that no matter what opposition I encountered, I was going to hang on to the altar of God until I touched the hem of Jesus' garment. No matter what it took, I was going to touch that robe for my son. The Bible proclaims, "By whose stripes ye were healed" (1 Peter 2:24).

I thank God that I had firsthand experience with the retarded even before my son was born. My oldest sister, Myrtle, was born severely retarded. I knew the heartache that filled our whole family and the helplessness that we felt. Her retardation was due to a birth defect. The distress of my mother over her retarded daughter and the drunkenness of my father were so great, that it is hard to imagine how she survived. My sister lived to be forty-nine, nine years longer than the doctors had predicted.

When Ricky was born, the doctors advised me that I would never raise him because he was too sickly. I said, "Yes, but the Lord God gave him to Elias and me. We will raise him." During the first six years of his life, we slept with an alarm clock going off every thirty minutes. One minute, Ricky would be all right and the next minute we would be on our way to the emergency room. We did not realize that our child was mentally disabled or retarded. He had severe brain damage and dyslexia. We did not know that, even with his disability, Satan would turn against him even more, throwing fiery darts of sickness upon him.

In particular, Ricky would endure terrible fevers and convulsions. It seemed that he suffered from sickness all the time. If he became excited or stressed-out, his sickness would become worse. Since he could be sick at any moment, we could not let him play like other children. It seemed as if little changes in our lives, like the weather or a cold, would bring on sickness. When his fever went above 101°, convulsions would also be present. Ricky could change from being physically well to being physically ill within seconds. From moment to moment, Elias and I never knew what would happen. We did not know whether we would have a normal day or spend all day and night at the hospital.

Satan again struck my son in a way that I never anticipated. One day Ricky woke up and was paralyzed, unable to walk. Our doctor examined him and said that there was nothing that could help. We fell upon our knees and cried out to God. At the end of three months Ricky experienced God's healing power and was able to walk. He was able to take small steps and then larger ones. Finally, within days, all the negative effects that he had suffered from that attack were gone. He could walk normally.

It was in the midst of crying over my son that I called my son's pediatrician, Dr. Frame, and asked him if I could come to the office to talk to him about Ricky. I was crying hysterically when I got to his office, feeling that I was a bad mother since my son could not stay well. The doctor was very kind and had a long talk with me. He suggested that Elias and I put down carpet all over the house so that our son would not be on the cold tile floors. We did that, but it did not seem to help. Ricky still had colds and sinus infections and suffered constantly with tonsillitis, bronchitis, ear inflammation and many other things. The first six years of his life seemed a constant battle against illness.

We had been to the hospital so many times that the nurses knew who we were and were ready for us when we came in. All that we knew to do was to stand and pray as Daniel did in Daniel 9. We had no idea about what was happening to us or why these calamities seemed to descend upon our small family. We were at the end of our hope, and our faith was stretched to its very limit. We had gone as far as we could physically go. When we reach this breaking point, God always steps into the picture.

Within the first six years of Ricky's life, God stepped into the picture in a particular and special manner. He sent an evangelist to Jacksonville when my son was about four years old who prayed that Ricky would sleep and be able to overcome his insomnia. We were used to Ricky sleeping for thirty minutes and being awake for eight hours or more. The only time that

Elias and I were able to sleep soundly and without worry during these times was when my mother-in-law would come down and take care of Ricky. She was a wonderful praying saint of God who prayed constantly for our son and his deliverance. Many more joined her in praying for a miracle for Ricky.

We began to realize that apart from God, we could do little to help Ricky. This sense of helplessness brought us to our knees. God led me into a season of intense intercession. To obey I had to be willing to eliminate everything that distracted me from perfect obedience.

As I was cooking supper one day, Ricky had a convulsion and fell out of his high chair onto our tile floor. I did not move him until my neighbor came and checked to see if any bones had been broken. Another time, I was tied up in traffic, and Ricky had a bad convulsion. All I could do was put my finger in his mouth to keep him from chewing his tongue until I could get him to a hospital. Elias and I never had any warning about his convulsions. Most of the time I was not alone when this happened. This was another evidence of God's mercy.

I remember the night he was going to graduate from kindergarten. Ricky had a double convulsion, and his face turned black. I thought I was going to lose him! Thank God for the doctor and the nurse that were there that night. Despite their skill, we all felt truly helpless. Medically, they could only treat the symptoms, but through prayer and the laying on of hands, God could heal him totally. He never had another seizure after that night.

As I look back, I realize that the wisest decision Elias and I ever made was to become Christians. I thought as a teenager that I needed Jesus, but I did not realize that I was going to need

Him even more for my son. Elias and I began to understand that we had to have more help, and that it had to come from God alone!

As Ricky continued to grow up physically, both Elias and I began to grow more serious about our relationship with Jesus. Everything that the world had to offer meant nothing to us. The significance of material things began fading into the shadows before the intense sorrow over our son. Even though I loved coaching my softball team, I gave it up to study the Word of God and stay in my prayer closet for my son.

Elias and I began to realize that our son was truly retarded when he entered kindergarten. It did not take us long to find out that he could not distinguish one letter from another. We became frantic that Ricky did not know the difference between letters. The kindergarten teacher tried to calm our concerns by pointing out that he was just a young five-year-old. I was to hear repeatedly, "Don't worry! He is just not old enough yet to learn." When Ricky began elementary school, the same statement was made in both the first and second grades. The teachers gave excuse after excuse about why Ricky could not learn. They accused him of suffering from excitability, anxiety and hyperactivity. None of these accusations were true. They did not have time to worry about one child among countless others in the classroom. One child falling through the cracks of the school system did not warrant their attention.

No matter what my husband and I did to help Ricky learn, it was unsuccessful. Yet, we continued to try. All through the second, third and fourth grades, we continued to try and teach the alphabet one letter at a time. We would write phrases on cards like, "Ricky and Snoopy" (his dog). As long as the cards were up, Ricky could repeat with us what was written on them. However, he could not pronounce any of the words or remember the phrases when the cards were taken down, hidden or covered. He would then begin to cry anew.

The next few years were no better. The school system and the teachers kept saying that Ricky had no learning problems. They passed him from grade to grade even though he could not read a simple word. One of my neighbors, Virginia Harrell, who was a substitute teacher, saw firsthand how the teachers treated my child. They did not encourage him to do anything. They would not even make him stand up for the pledge of allegiance. They gave up on him. But, thank God, we did not! But what is even more important is that God never gave up on Ricky!

Ricky was just sitting in the classroom, taking up space. The teachers did not know what to do when I would go to talk to any of them. I even asked the school to have him tested repeatedly. The absence of concern on the part of the school system exasperated me. I felt that they had turned their back on my child. Because I was so concerned about my son, I made an appointment with the guidance clinic through the school board. The specialists kept Ricky for about three hours testing him. They called me with good news. Though he could not read a word or a letter, they concluded that he was mentally normal. They implied that I was too overprotective. They wanted to punish him for not learning. This I would not allow.

While I am not a doctor or psychologist, I believe that the spirit of my son knew that something was wrong with his brain. He seemed to intuitively understand that he was not like other children. We would catch him sitting and crying by himself many times. Ricky even resorted to paying other children to play games with him.

I decided that I needed to do whatever I had to do, to get help for Ricky. We hired tutors and placed our son in a learning institution that dealt with children who have learning difficulties. One of these institutions was known as Reading Researcher Institution and was headed by Dr. Skinner. We still have the canceled checks proving that Ricky did enter this institution.

Ricky attended another institution that has long since ceased its operation. One day he tried to run away, slamming into a glass door so hard that it almost broke. The teachers there were constantly yelling, and Ricky couldn't take it anymore. After this, Ricky came very close to having a nervous breakdown. His father found him shaking uncontrollably while trying to crawl under a car. Elias picked him up, wrapped his arms around him, and said, "Ricky, whether you ever learn or not, your mother and I love you. We will work and save for you." When they came through the door, I turned off dinner, took him in my arms, and said the same thing that Elias had said. We all cried together.

I finally sought help through the pediatrician who had worked with us for so long in dealing with Ricky's problems. I told him my fears and my belief that Ricky suffered from a form of learning disability known as dyslexia. He informed me that he believed that his son also had dyslexia. He shared that he had sent his son to a leading specialist in Gainesville. He sent us there.

The doctor and his staff spent three days testing and analyzing Ricky. At our consultation, the doctor called us in to tell us that Ricky not only had dyslexia, but severe brain damage as well. There was nothing more that he could do medically.

Ricky, according to this specialist, could never learn anything. In addition to his three close calls with a nervous breakdown, his IQ was extremely low. He would never be able to live anything close to a normal life. As he said this, the Holy Spirit rose up within me and prayed, "No! He won't! For as long as Jesus Christ sits at the right hand of the Father, my son will never go through life like that. I asked God for the gift of a son, and my Father knows how to give only good gifts to his people."

The specialist stayed with us for four hours, teaching us ways to deal with Ricky. We were unaware that Ricky was outside the room listening to all of this. Can you imagine what he must have felt upon hearing that nothing could ever be done for him?

Leaving Gainesville to come home was the loneliest time that Elias and I ever spent. We had hit rock bottom. During the trip back home I sat very quietly with my arms around Ricky and spoke few words. When we finally arrived home, we made a covenant with the Lord. We gave the Lord everything we had. We cleaned out our bank account and gave it all to God. We dedicated our son to God, acknowledging that we did not have the ability to raise him in our own strength. In essence, we gave God our whole lives and began living a new life with God at the core. Both Elias and I began a life of fasting and prayer, seeking God to be over our child and over our lives.

It was during this intense fire of suffering that we experienced God's purifying power working in all of us. Until that point in our lives, I can truthfully say that I had never been completely sold-out to God. I paid the preacher to read the Bible, understand its mysteries, and do the praying for the congregation and for the nation. God showed us how false this way of thinking is. God has called each of us to get into His Word and apply it for ourselves. We can't depend on someone to do it for us.

Elias and I began to study the Bible, researching it and studying church history and theology. We began to teach Ricky what the Bible said about faith, prayer and healing. As we put him to bed at night, I would read the Bible and pray with him. I would tell him that God loved him and wanted to heal him. I would quote Scriptures on healing from the books of Isaiah and James.

We did not know at the time that Ricky was praying as well. After Elias and I would return to our room, Ricky would cover his head and pray that God would heal him and make him like other children. Ricky frequently asked, "Lord, why can't I be healed and be like other children?" When we found his pillow wet with tears, he admitted that he also had been crying aloud to God for his healing. It was so heartbreaking to see our son crying out to God with so much anguish and pain. He was retarded, yet his spirit knew what was going on and how hurt he felt by the children who taunted him. Ricky did not realize that he had entered into a life of prayer where patience is practiced, learned and understood.

Ricky continued to pray, just as his father and I did. Our faith and our prayer life were all that we had. During those painful years, I prayed day and night, weeping before the Lord God for my son. Though I did not consciously understand intercessory prayer, I was practicing it.

In 1973, Ricky still attended public school. He continued to be passed from one grade to another, until as a sixth grader he could not spell or write his name. At this time, Virginia Harrell again came to our rescue. She knew that the public school that

Ricky attended was doing nothing for him. One evening she came to our house to tell us that University Christian School had a special education class with only ten pupils. She thought this would be a good place for Ricky since the teacher was trained to help disabled children.

The morning that I took Ricky to register was a very bad day. He pitched a fit about leaving the public school for University Christian. I would drive a few miles, pull over and offer to carry Ricky back to the other school. I made it clear that he had to go to school somewhere. At last, I pulled the car off the road and sat and cried. When Ricky saw how painful all this was for me, he agreed to go to the new school.

When Ricky was tested, the teachers found out that, although he was twelve years old, he was mentally below a kindergarten level. Even though his academic level was too low, God made an opening for him in that class. As he began attending, the school helped all it could. However, there seemed to be very little that anyone could do for him. I still took him to tutors weekly. In the summer I began again trying to teach him at least one hundred words. Elias and I increased our prayers for him and took him to every preacher who believed in healing by prayer and the laying on of hands.

Ricky's frustration level seemed to ease at this school. He cried less and even enjoyed the bus ride to school. Ricky continued to be teased and laughed at by other children because of his disability. He was called many names that made fun of him, even though the school included the special education children in everything. For example, at Christmas the school had made a place in the Christmas program for all the kids. That night was so special for all the parents to see their children having a good time. Ricky played the prophet Isaiah in this Christmas program, foretelling the coming of the Messiah.

From 1973 to the fall of 1977, Ricky saw little success in learning. Within this time period he did advance slowly to a third grade level. No further advancement or improvement was predicted for Ricky. He seemed to have reached the highest level he could attain. We three continued to hold on to God even though Satan seemed to be winning the battle in Ricky's life. Then God gave us an early Christmas present that we will never forget.

CHAPTER 3

Cost of a Miracle

During this time Satan struck against us from other directions with other storms. Our lives became complicated as Satan and his forces sought our destruction. More than ever, it became apparent that the goal of these tribulations was to prevent us from effectively battling for our son. Their purpose was to tie us down, weaken us and turn our attention away from the miracle that waited.

The first of these storms came against my sister Myrtle who lived in Douglas, Georgia. She was having surgery for intestinal cancer and was not expected to live. My family called to ask if I could come and help them. I had been through a bad car wreck and my doctor would not allow me to drive. The Lord provided a friend who drove me to see Myrtle and her family for a week. I felt like a yo-yo being pulled in many directions at the same time. The situation with Ricky, my sister in the hospital, Elias, my job and other things all combined simultaneously to tear me apart.

When I went to Augusta and found the weakened condition of my sister, I cried. In addition to her cancer surgery she had also had a colostomy redone. This second surgery made things worse instead of better. She was hanging between death and life. My other sister Ruby came to be with me, and we were so upset by the suffering our sister went through. She had such a high fever that she lay on a sheet of ice. She stayed frozen to the bed with her internal temperature constantly monitored. Ruby would take the day shift while I would take the night shift. We also hired a private nurse around the clock to help us. But our sister knew when we were in the room. If we left, her blood pressure shot up. Though she was out of it and mentally disabled, her spirit knew we were present and our hands were always upon her.

One night she was so out of it because of her high fever, I sat on the bed with my hand on her until the early morning. She began to pray the most beautiful prayer of repentance that I have ever heard in my life. She spoke words that were not in her limited vocabulary. I knew that the Holy Spirit was guiding her spirit to pray this prayer. God was allowing me to witness this awesome experience and was giving me the assurance that she was saved. Immediately, I remembered the promise that Jesus had made to me that He would save my family. The tears began to flow down my cheeks! I could not hold it in any longer as the realization of the fulfillment of God's Word hit me. Soon after Christmas, Myrtle died. I was at peace knowing that her spirit was in the hands of the Lord and that one day I would see her in Heaven, gloriously perfect.

My mother was the next person in my family that Satan attacked. She had gone to see one of my sisters and while there, a blood vessel burst in her stomach. My sister called and asked me to come and help her. We put her in the hospital even though she had no insurance. We agreed to be responsible for her bill and were worried about paying for it. The Lord provided us with a doctor that gave us a discount for both the hospital and his cost.

Some families seem to have someone who is considered the "black sheep" of the family. They go their own way and make their own rules. My sister Sue fit that description in our family. She appeared to be more like my father than the rest of his children. She was stubborn, prideful, rebellious and demanding. She loved material things and all that the world offered. My sister loved the party life, drinking, dancing and committing all sorts of evil affairs.

This was her attitude and way of thinking until she became so depraved that she destroyed herself and her family. Sue thought herself unable to give up the world and tried to find some type of Christianity that would fit her lifestyle and satisfy her soul. She tried the Jehovah Witnesses and accepted that life for a while because they taught against the doctrine of hell. Gradually she began to see that there was a real hell, not just a hell upon this earth. She saw the reality of the supernatural when she allowed a witch to live in her home. She saw firsthand the power of Satan as the witch cast spells and did incantations.

I remember that when her daughter was about three, Sue and her husband went to dinner in a restaurant with her. The waiter asked the daughter, "What would you like?"The daughter replied, "A beer." Both Sue and her husband thought it was funny. However, it was not funny at all when their daughter grew up. The seeds of destruction had been planted within their child, and she became extremely rebellious. She took countless kinds of drugs, drank excessively and led a promiscuous and reckless life. Sue's family lost everything that they had spent a lifetime working for. They had experienced financial blessing and bought all that they could buy. Only happiness eluded them. By the time she accepted the Lord, it was too late for God to give her back what Satan had stolen.

One evening the Spirit of the Lord came upon me to pray for Sue and her family after they left my home to return to theirs. "Likewise the Spirit also helps in our weaknesses. For we do not know what we should pray for as we ought, but the Spirit Himself makes intercession for us with groanings which cannot be uttered. Now He who searches the hearts knows what the mind of the Spirit is, because He makes intercession for the saints according to the will of God" (Romans 8: 26–27, NKJV).

After two hours, I called their home and shared with them that the Lord had directed me to pray for their survival of a car wreck. Immediately, Sue told me that they had been in a bad wreck with a log truck and some people had been killed. No one there could understand how Sue and her husband had survived. The importance of following the leading of the Holy Spirit hit home. Satan had set a trap for my sister's family, but God delivered them. Despite God's intervention in her life, my sister continued down her path of destruction.

Watching people that you care about destroy themselves is very hard. I tried to get Sue help in various ways. Instead of thanking me for helping her and her family, she carried a loaded pistol around her home for about five weeks waiting for me to come in so that she could "blow my brains out" (as she termed it). But the Lord protected me and kept her from using it. Her husband even told a friend that if anyone discussed "that Jesus junk" in his store, he would demand that the person not come back.

My sister was at my house preparing to go to the hospital for her fifteenth surgery. She hated me so much that she said, "I would rather die and go to hell than to be in your home and have you help me." It seemed that I could see the very hatred of Satan for me in her eyes. Satan said through her, "I hate your guts." I said, "Yes, little sister I know, but I love you." I knew that God would separate us for my protection and the protection of my family. I began to cry in agony over this.

While in my home, the demons within her began to manifest themselves right before me as her voice and her face changed. I will never forget their evil voices. The words that came out of her mouth were not her words but Satan's. I had allowed her to be in our home because I knew that the Lord would protect us. The Lord revealed to me that she wanted to kill herself. I lay on the floor in front of her bedroom door so that she could not leave to get a knife or other weapon with which to harm herself. I did not realize that she had sleeping pills with her. But God only allowed her to put the pills up to her mouth before she froze. She could not actually put them in her mouth because of God's intervention.

After that long night, I got up to fix her a good breakfast. When I came back from putting gas in the car, she had the worst look on her face. She had been notified that her husband had died, and she was in shock. I went back to her house to stay with her during his funeral. Having to leave my home and stay with my sister during this time was an experience that I will never forget. There was no place, I believe, more demonic than this home. The demons of hell could literally be heard, yelling, howling and screaming. I could hear the gnashing of teeth. The evil whispering that these spirits spoke so penetrated the atmosphere of that home, that I could only stay there by pleading the blood of Jesus over me. While my other sisters took sleeping pills to fall asleep, I remained vigilant. I felt that it was not a time for sleep but for battle. I learned firsthand about the power of the blood over every other weapon of our spiritual warfare.

The Lord became so close to me during this time. He would reveal to Elias and me things that were going to happen to our family. One night the Lord showed me that there would be an attempted shooting of my sister Sue at noon the next day. Immediately, I began to pray. But this time I prayed more powerfully than I have ever done. As I was praying, Satan spoke to me and said, "She will die tomorrow!" I told Satan, "No! As God liveth, she will not die!" I claimed her for the kingdom of God and pled the blood of Jesus over her repeatedly.

The day of my sister's attempted shooting was a terrible day. Shortly after noon, my extension at work rang with an emergency telephone call. Sue had been shot at six times but was never hit. I decided that she was not going to go to hell if I could help it. I decided to pray and fast until God moved somehow and saved her. Having no theology to discredit what God could do or what He had spoken to me, I believed in the promise God made to me. I held on to it with a death grip.

Sue suffered many debilitating problems, physical, mental and spiritual. After her husband died, the doctor found a spur growing on her spinal cord. The pain was so great that she became more dependent on drugs and alcohol. This was the only time that she experienced relief from the pain. Despite this, she tried her best to keep the business going and deal with her daughter the best way she knew how.

Her daughter married and this positively affected her behavior. She was a great wife to her husband. She would have his breakfast fixed even if she had to get up at four o'clock in the morning. She had his clothes washed and ironed. After she had their child, her husband left her. From that point on, she fell deeper and deeper into the arms of Satan and his kind of life, indulging in all kinds of sin and becoming violent. She married someone else and became pregnant with his child.

There were times when my niece was so intoxicated or on drugs that she would try to kill her husband, her mother, myself or anyone else. She stabbed her second husband, and when he was recovering in the hospital, she pulled the tubes out of him. People literally became terrified of her.

With all of these problems, my sister never took any blame for how her daughter had turned out. I wish that my sister could have lived long enough to see her daughter change, becoming a loving person and marrying a man that loved her.

One of the last times I talked to Sue and her daughter, Sue said, "I was not a good mother, but I am a wonderful grandmother." She no longer wanted to live the kind of life that sowed so many seeds of destruction. In the last years of her life, paralyzed and suffering from a stroke, she wanted Jesus. She called out to Jesus for mercy. The Lord Himself heard her cries and in a vision came down to her. She saw Him in this vision, walking into her room and telling her how long she had to live. That night she accepted the Lord. The hatred, bitterness and stubbornness melted away and what was left behind was a sweet and loving person who loved Jesus. What I saw God doing before my eyes took forty long years of fasting and prayer to be accomplished. God kept His Word, but I did my part! From that night on she continued to say, "He's real! He's real! He's real!" Jesus became the beginning, the middle and the end of her speech. She ate, lived and slept the Word of God. She was never the same again, and God continued to keep His Word about my family.

Sue was finally put into a nursing home where I could go see about her without worrying about running into her daughter who always picked a fight. She only weighed sixty pounds. After working all day and driving about sixty miles to my job, I would run home, cook dinner and drive the same distance to feed her. It took about two hours to feed her, one bite at a time. Soon after moving into the nursing home, she died and met the Master she so longed to see.

Next, the Lord began to deal with Elias about his younger brother, Wallace, a deputy sheriff in Coffee County, Georgia. God gave Elias a vision that his brother was going to be shot with his own gun within six months. He told a pastor about what God had shown him and sought immediate prayer for his brother. The pastor anointed a handkerchief for my husband to carry with him to Georgia. When Elias and I arrived to meet Wallace, he told us that as we were praying for him, he was jumping down two flights of stairs to get away from a .38 pistol. We did not feel like this was the incident that God had warned us about. We gave him the handkerchief that had been anointed and told him that we were praying and would continue to pray for him.

One hour before the end of the six months, Wallace was shot with his own gun. At the same time, Elias was crying out to God for mercy. When I came home from work that morning, Elias was looking out the window and saying, "God does not lie. Last night Wallace was shot in the chest. God spoke to me and said, 'Since you have given to Me both your life and your finances, I am giving back to you. Your brother will be all right.'"

When Elias went to the hospital, he was allowed to see his brother. Wallace told Elias that what the Lord had foretold had happened. Two weeks later, Wallace was in our home telling us about what had happened to him as he was shot. The bullet had entered between the two main arteries of the heart. He said that as he died, he left his body. He then saw the ambulance that had been called and knew who came into his house to help him. He rode with his body to the hospital. He saw the doctor and nurse run out to meet the ambulance and remembered what they said. But what is even more dramatic is the fact that he saw the very hand of God come down from Heaven, hit his chest while the nurse screamed out loud, "I have a pulse!" All the damage caused by the bullet was instantaneously healed. Instead of weeks of recuperation, he needed none. That is just like God!

I would like to tell you that his life changed because of that experience, but it didn't happen. God gave him chance after chance, and he rebuffed them all. For the sake of Elias, God spared Wallace, but instead of changing, he fell deeper and deeper into sin. Does not the Bible say that the wages of sin are death? Twenty years later, he committed suicide with the same kind of gun with which he was shot the first time and in the same place. What a tragedy!

Another turning point in my life and the lives of my family was the death of my sister Ruby. When I heard about her death, I cried bitter tears to God. I wondered why God allowed her to die because I needed her so badly. Ruby had always been the one constant in our family, helping anyone who needed her. She had been of great help to our mother. Since I lived in Jacksonville and could only go up to Georgia occasionally, she stayed near my mother and took care of her.

Before her death, one of the greatest events in her life was the baptism of the Holy Spirit with speaking in tongues. She had always wondered about speaking in tongues, questioning whether they were biblical and whether they were for this day. All of this came to a head one day when my sister and I were in the field picking butter beans. The Lord showed me a vision that someone in our family would die. Right there I began to cry out to God for help and mercy and began to speak in tongues. Ruby was shocked, awed and worried. She had never heard anything like that. She could say nothing but, "Baby, please get a hold of yourself! You are going to have a nervous breakdown!" I said, "Sis, can't you understand what this family is about to go through? We need to get a hold of God!"

After I left her house, she fell upon her knees and cried out to God saying, "God, if speaking in tongues is real, I want it!" Then, the power of the Holy Spirit came over her and she began to speak the words of a language that she didn't know. She had never expected so much joy and peace, unknown to her and unexplainable! She received this gift three years before she died and never wanted to lose it.

After this, we were able to pray together in a completeness and power that both of us had never experienced before. Although I had experienced the baptism of the Holy Spirit years before she received it, I had not experienced this level of holiness and power. According to Deuteronomy 32:30, two can put to flight at least ten thousand. This was the first time in our family that two Spirit-filled saints were joined in the battle against the forces of evil for our family. There was another sister who was Spirit-filled, but she lived far away from the family and could not always join in the struggle.

While Ruby and I were winning the battle for our family against Satan, God warned me that Satan desired the life of my sister Ruby. I stayed on my knees and prayed using the passage about Hezekiah seeking God for mercy and protection. (See 2 Kings 20:1.) God graciously moved and her life was extended for a considerable time.

Nonetheless, there are times when no one can stand up for you in spiritual warfare, you must fight alone. While my sister Ruby was Spirit-filled, she did not know or comprehend that she was in danger and needed to fight against the wiles of Satan. I warned her that she was under direct attack by witchcraft, but she would not listen. When God warns us and we don't listen, the results can be terrible and disastrous. I believe that she succumbed to the plans of Satan and died before her time. God allowed it even though it wasn't His original intention.

My son explains the fulfillment of God's Word and His intentions in connection to free will in this way:

> The fulfillment of God's Word and God's intention is not placed outside the sphere of human freedom and choice, and most often is dependent upon free moral agents to become fulfilled. It is grace that demands that the intentions of God must allow free moral agents a choice to accept or reject God's will for their lives. When God uses a choice done by free-will agents, He works to turn the actions of men and other creatures into a method or means by which His plans may be fulfilled. In other

words, He takes those actions that are contrary to His will and takes hold of the consequences and changes things so that they may be beneficial to the fulfillment of His plans.

The day I learned that my sister Ruby had died, I lost it. I went into shock. I could not believe that God would do this to me. I cried out loudly and bitterly while walking throughout the house, yelling, "God, what are You doing to me? Do You love me? Didn't You know that the family needed her? Why have You forsaken me?" I felt that I needed her so badly to go with me through our family troubles and to give me courage. We were such a comfort to each other and could cry on one another's shoulders. She was the very heart of our family. That night I walked in the backyard asking God why. It seemed that God was a thousand miles away and had turned His face from me. It is such an awful feeling to feel that God has forsaken you! My life, which was already shaken, became worse and the storms of life seemed to rage around me more heavily.

Elias did not say anything about the death of Ruby until we were on our way to the funeral. I still could not say anything except, "Why, God, why?" Elias was the one that God enlightened and gave the reasons for her death. Elias simply said that God did not tell me about her death because I would have prayed and fasted until He would have spared her again. It was not my time to do this, but it was time for Ruby to step up and heed the warnings of the Lord. In addition, he said that my mother was another reason that God allowed this. God would work through this to save her.

In the midst of Ruby's funeral preparations, I was wondering what my family and I were going to do about

Mother. Mother had burned herself very badly three days before Ruby died. I had told Ruby then that Mother was unable to live by herself due to her age and health. The day of Ruby's funeral, my family and I had to put Mother in the hospital for a skin graft on her arm. This was a terrible time. Ruby's death and my mother's accident had upset me so much. Then I found out that my mother had cancer of the liver and would not live long. I went to my car and began to cry out to God saying, "Lord, You promised me that You will not let more be put on me than I can bear" (1 Corinthians 10:13). Immediately, the Lord spoke to me saying, "Go on a five-day fast." I began to fast and a few of the nurses joined me. Three days after I completed the five-day fast, the doctor came into her room and said that he wanted to send her to another hospital for a CAT scan. At that time not all hospitals had this equipment. From Thursday through Saturday morning, the hospital ran tests. Finally, the doctor came into the room a little disturbed and bewildered. He simply said, "I do not know what to tell you about your mother. Other doctors and I have consulted together about the diagnosis and have come to the conclusion that your mother had liver cancer, but now her liver is as normal as yours and mine. I don't know what happened." I said, "Doctor, do you believe in fasting and praying?" He said, "Yes!" I said, "Doctor, God put me on a fast for this healing!" He told me to take her home.

This was the beginning of nine years of what can only be called "hell." It was overwhelming because I was still dealing with a retarded son and a mother who seemed truly demon-possessed.

My mother was the hardest person to take care of that anyone had ever seen. I entered into a time of intercessory prayer more intense than any I had ever experienced.

After my sister Ruby's death, I had a vision in which the Lord carried me away into hell. I fell down deeper and deeper into a deep pit. This falling lasted for a considerable length of time. When I arrived in hell, there was darkness everywhere; yet, there was a light in the midst of that darkness. I assumed that the light must have been the light of God shining even in hell itself. It must have been the Shekinah Glory, the divine presence of the Lord being manifested. This light penetrated far enough for me to see what was going on. Though I did not literally see the dead, I saw the shadows or forms of many in hell. I saw the shapes of some that I knew did not live a holy life and were already dead. God was telling me that they had gone to hell. I saw the forms of people who were still living. I knew God was telling me that they were destined for hell if they did not change. One of these was my mother. I saw her form hanging and looking over hell. I felt that this meant that she would go to hell if she did not change. When I saw her form, I cried out to God, "Don't let her go to hell! Her life has been so hard!"

After this vision, I ran into the living room and told my husband what had happened. He said that my mother was not saved. The whole purpose of the vision was to warn me that my mother did not yet belong to God. She had lived as a hypocrite for many years, going to church though she was not saved. She knew about Jesus, but had never met Him. My dilemma was how to get my mother to realize that she was not saved.

Three weeks later, a tent revival came to Jacksonville. All of us, including my mother, went. The preacher, whom we had never seen before, said to me, "I am going to eat breakfast with you in the morning." He later told Elias that my mother had to repent of her sins, especially sins that she believed God would never forgive. He came to our home and talked to her personally and privately. While she was still not saved, this was the beginning of her deliverance. As in the early church, some are delivered from demon possession in stages. I think that this was a clear example of this. The early church said that until one is completely delivered from demonic possession, that person could not be saved.

I wish I could say that the preacher's talk to her was all that it took for her to have peace and be saved, but Satan did not want to give her up. A major battle was still going on. Elias and I had to live in intercessory prayer, learning even more deeply how to pray more fervently. Intercessory prayer became not only a ministry, but also a way of life. We learned that it can be a vehicle to really touch the heart of God. It will open doors that nothing else can open; it will bring down strongholds when nothing else can break them; it will help win the battle for our souls. Intercessory prayer, equipped with the baptism of the Holy Spirit and the evidence of speaking in tongues, will empower the saint of God like nothing else. Intercessory prayer and tears are interwoven. Tears touch God when nothing else can because they are linked to intense prayer.

Elias, Ricky and I finally found out what was troubling Mother. First, we saw three demons come out of her, each looking like a black cat. Another night we heard a horrible scream come from her room. My son and I ran into her room as she was screaming, "Get those babies off me and my bed!"

I wondered what had happened in her life to torment her so. In addition to being retarded, my sister Myrtle was not able to walk early in her life, and everything that she ate had to be cooked for three hours. It was so much work for Mother to take care of her in addition to her other children. Mother was afraid of having other retarded children, and when she became pregnant twice again, she made herself have two miscarriages. For all these years, she had carried the guilt of those horrible acts. This led to nervous problems and several nervous breakdowns, including a stay in the mental hospital. She was under a doctor's care for years. How Satan tormented her and made her think that God would not forgive her for what she had done. What a burden she carried all those years!

During the time of caring for my mother, I reached my greatest point of despair and fatigue, even wishing to die. Even people in the Bible, on occasions, wished to die. Remember Jonah saying, "And it came to pass, when the sun did arise, that God prepared a vehement east wind; and the sun beat upon the head of Jonah, that he fainted, and wished in himself to die, and said, 'It is better for me to die than to live'" (Jonah 4:8).

During these years of hell, Mother always wanted to be right under my feet. Even while she was in the hospital, I had to stay with her. She tried to dominate my life and the lives of Elias and Ricky.

One cold day in January my mother had been acting nervously, walking the floor and becoming mentally unstable. She came to my bedroom at eight in the morning. The woman who had helped us with Mother for five years arrived at our home at 8:15 a.m. Between 8:00 a.m. and 8:15 a.m. my mother left the house, entered the backyard, walked to the creek, jumped in, came back to the house and was at our door waiting for this woman to come. When the aide came in, my wet and muddy mother walked behind her. My mother admitted that she had tried to commit suicide by jumping into the creek behind our house. She said that every time she would put her head under the water, an angel of God would physically jerk her head back up. She tried to kill herself several times and every time the angel of God would prevent it. My mother was quite old and unable to climb up and over the bulkhead that was placed between the creek and our backyard. Doing that would have been impossible for her apart from divine assistance.

What could I do? I put her into the bathtub with warm water and washed her. Then, I walked down behind the house to look. I saw where she had come out. I saw that the rocks and the cement of the bulkhead were still wet and muddy. How could I have ever gotten over her drowning? How messed up and sickly she had to be to do this to herself! I called the doctor and took her to the hospital. The doctor discovered that medication had caused her to become very unstable mentally.

In those years my mother frequently would be rushed to the hospital, especially for heart failure. She had been at death's door more times than can be counted. Doctors repeatedly thought that she would not make it out of the hospital. Yet, she always did.

One time when she became very sick, we brought her to the hospital and for three days I took care of her every minute. I did this so much that I did not have time for coffee or sleep. During these three days, she continued to cough and have diarrhea. My mother became so sick that I was forced to hold her on the bed and keep the IV in her arm.

At the end of the third day, the doctor came into my mother's room and told me that he could not find out what was wrong with her. He could not help her. Whatever was wrong or whatever type of sickness she had seemed to be killing her. Again I cried out to God. The Lord told me that it was a bird fever and gave me the name for it. I told the doctor what God had said. The doctor looked at me very strangely, turned around and hurried out. About one hour later he came back into the room and said that he did not have time to check out that she had bird fever, but that she had all the symptoms. Because she was dying, he had no time to run the necessary tests. I said, "Go ahead and treat her for that and I will take the responsibility!" He had to quarantine us. The Lord finally delivered my mother from the bird fever a few days later. I was exhausted after this stage of the battle, but the fight for my mother was still not over.

Satan, knowing that I could go no further, prompted my sister Sue to call the hospital and curse me for everything in the book. Finally, I knew that I could go no further. So again I began to cry out to God, "What is wrong that I have to go through this by myself? Lord, I can't go another night without sleep!" The Lord spoke and said, "You have not because you ask not!" It did not take me long to ask Him for help. In about ten minutes, the telephone rang with a friend calling to see if I needed help.

Mother got to where she would suffer insomnia until about five o'clock in the morning. During this time, she would call out all night long. Elias and I began to pray about that. We would go into her room and cry out to God for her night after night.

Nevertheless, it seemed that we would get through one thing only to be faced with another.

All of this was going on while Elias and I cried out to God for our son's healing as well. We also went anywhere that a revival was taking place so that godly men or women who had the gifts of the Holy Spirit working through them could pray for Ricky. I wanted someone to touch God for our son. Money and denominations don't matter when you need something from God badly enough.

The barrage of problems that Satan instigated within both our families became so horrible that they literally began to destroy all hope for our son to be healed. Satan's purpose was to tie Elias and me down, weaken us so that our attention was turned away from the miracle that awaited our son. These storms were causing so much destruction that God commanded that their interference be brought to an end. They were impeding my progress on my journey to touch God's heart for my son.

This all came to a head one night when the Lord spoke to me while I was in the lab at my work. He said to me, "Put thy family on the altar and leave them there!" I was not ready to let my family go to hell. I was going to press through to God. I was going to plead with God. I was going to argue with God until He moved. But when He told me to put my family on the altar and leave them there, I searched the Scriptures. I found Matthew 7:7–8, about continuing to knock until we receive what we ask. I prayed this back to God. But I told God that if He would confirm this in another way, I would do the best I could to lay them on the altar and leave them there. Don't ever say that to God unless you are ready for something to happen!

Approximately one week after that, I went to hear a minister, W. V. Grant, Sr., who came into Jacksonville to preach on the battle of Armageddon. I was especially interested in this subject and had done a lot of research on it. I really wanted to hear this man and what he had to say. I went over to the church that night and saw nearly two hundred people outside the church that could not even get in. All at once, a man took me by the elbow and led me through the crowd into the church. He sat me down in the second row, right on the aisle. I looked around the church to see if any older people were standing around, intending to give my seat to them, but something stronger than myself kept me in my seat. When the minister came to the platform, he said, "I said I was going to preach on the battle of Armageddon if the Lord let me! Yet, God changed my text when I came into this church! It is for this young lady sitting right here! I am going to teach you how to pray tonight! God has called you to be an intercessor! He called you to pray for other people! He loves someone else besides you and your bunch! He wants you to put your family on the altar and leave them there!"

God had done what I had asked Him to do. He had confirmed what He wanted me to do. Have you ever laid someone on the altar when Satan was trying to kill him or her? Have you ever had to sit back and watch God work instead of getting involved? I did not quite understand what the Lord meant at first about laying them on the altar and leaving them there. I remember many days and nights when I would have to hang up the telephone. I did not know what to do and neither did I know what was happening. There had been one thing after another in our lives for so long. So much horror had taken place that when the telephone rang, I began to tremble. I would then hang the telephone up, go back, lie on the bed and weep violently. I finally understood that by placing my family upon the altar, I was surrendering them into God's hands and turning my attention firmly toward praying for my son first and then others.

These were just some of the storms we had to endure. Always one problem would begin before another problem ended. There was never a time that could be considered a time of peace. At these times I would pray and be led into fasts from three to twenty-one days in order to break through the barriers of the demonic. Praying and fasting helped! Apart from both praying and fasting, we might not have survived to tell the history of our lives and relate what God has done.

CHAPTER 4

Receiving a Miracle

In 1975 I experienced something beyond expectation that was humbling and yet almost indescribable. I was praying on my knees in our extra room, which had become our prayer room. Nothing was out of the ordinary until I felt the Spirit of God rush into the room and overshadow me. Then, I was given a vision. I saw one of the same wheels that Ezekiel described in the first and tenth chapters of Ezekiel. This wheel-angel came rolling into my room early in the morning. The wheel was actually a type of angel, sent by God to deliver a message of hope and promise. This angel broke through the demonic layers that bound and imprisoned us.

The angel appeared as a wheel within a wheel. He had the appearance of an inner and outer wheel attached by a joint to make one individual wheel. There were four sides and the angel could go in any direction he chose without turning. His color was that of amber. The rings of the wheel were full of eyes. The angel had the ability to speak, and his voice was as the voice of many waters all sounding in sequence. The glory of God that surrounded him lit up the room. While I had envisioned angels before this event, I had never seen any like this. I have never forgotten it. The entire miracle of my son's healing is founded upon this vision. It became our lifeline because all that God gave to us afterward was used to confirm this vision.

In the midst of this, I saw a sickle in a large wheat field cutting down wheat even though no one was operating it. There were large storehouses that were being filled to the brim. The angel spoke to me and said, "The wheat field is the world of sinners; the sickle going about cutting down the wheat is the End-Time harvest. The storehouses are the churches who are alive, giving the Holy Spirit a place in their services. These storehouses will be filled to the brim." I felt that the Lord, through His angel, promised another Great Awakening in the End Times, which would take place before the Rapture of the church.

Since I was not a biblical scholar, I did not understand the "wheel" when I saw it. I did not know that it was a very powerful angel, or that Ezekiel had seen four of these wheels himself more than 2,500 years ago. I was truly upset, not knowing whether I was crazy or moving into the realm of fanaticism. The church that I attended, though believing in the gifts of the Holy Spirit, visions, dreams and other manifestations, had not been taken as deeply as I was going.

I prayed for help and God led me to call my sister-in-law, Evelyn Roberts Cox. She was, and still is, a Church of God minister. When I told her what had happened, she informed me that what I had seen was found in the Bible. I had unknowingly explained the wheel exactly as Ezekiel had seen it. I was confused and asked her why the angel had also shown me a man and said, "This is for you," when I already had a husband. She told me that this was not what the wheel angel meant. She said, "Hold on to the Lord, let nothing divert you from the goal set before you by God. Whatever was going on was truly of God so that you would hang on." She also said to wait and allow God to unravel the mystery about the man. I waited and within three weeks what the angel had spoken about a man did come to pass.

On Sunday, at the last point of this three-week period, I could hardly contain myself. I could not be still! It felt as if I had fire in my bones. Did not Jeremiah say, "His Word was in mine heart as a burning fire shut up in my bones, and I was weary with forbearing, and I could not stay" (Jeremiah 20:9)?

I tried to read a Christian book, and the more I read, the more I would burn, and then the more nervous I would be. It was so bad that Elias told me to go to the hospital to find out what was going on. None of the doctors or the nurses could find anything wrong with me and sent me home. As I drove home, I turned on the radio and heard an advertisement about a tent revival taking place nearby that night. As I was listening to the radio, I felt the Lord's call to go.

When I got there, standing on the platform was the man I had seen in the vision three weeks earlier. Then he took the microphone and said, "My meeting here in Jacksonville is over." I thought to myself that I had just gotten there. Then, the evangelist said, "A prophet is coming into Jacksonville and will use my tent to hold a revival. If this man tells you that you are going to die, you better make your funeral arrangements!" The prophet was Billy Jo Fain, a former bank robber who had been on the FBI's ten most wanted list. The evangelist continued by saying that this man had been tried and sentenced to a ninety-nine year prison sentence. Yet his praying mother cried out to God, reminding Him that even before his birth her son had been called to be a prophet. She cried out to God that the life he was living was not what was promised. Miraculously, God set this man free from his term and he became a minister for God.

When it was time for the evangelist to pray for people, he called me up out of the audience and told me to lay hands upon others. Later, he told me that he saw from the pulpit that I was engulfed in a flame of fire and needed to pray for the people there who were in need. I found out that praying for people was the only way the anointing of God could be released within me and its power diminished within my bones. The fire that I was feeling was God's anointing that needed an outlet. I had never been taught that the anointing needs a channel for release. This release comes only by praying for others, especially with the laying on of hands. When I prayed for others, the burning lessened and would stop temporarily. It would then come back as God directed me to pray for more people.

I came home and told Elias and Ricky what had happened. Elias immediately said, "There will be false prophets before the End Time deceiving many! We must guard ourselves against all deception! We will not go!" I spoke to him very calmly and said, "You may not go, but the Lord is dealing with me. I am going!" When it comes right down to it, we must obey God rather than men. Peter and the other apostles had to make that same choice. Acts 5:29 says, "We ought to obey God rather than men." Elias had not seen the vision and did not have the conviction of the Holy Spirit to go to the tent revival. He was worried about me going off the deep end, following false prophets and false teachers. We finally agreed to "lay out a fleece" before God as the saints in the Old Testament had done when they did not know the exact will of God for themselves or their nation. (See

Deuteronomy 18:4; Judges 6:37–40; Job 31:20.) We prayed that if this prophet was from God, he would call all three of us out at once and pray for us. Since I had never seen that happen before, it seemed like a good test to determine whether he was of God or not.

On a Wednesday morning, Billy Jo Fain had his first service in that old tent. I drove there in a separate car from Elias and Ricky. All three of us sat in different locations inside. We were "trying the spirits," just as John had warned all saints to do. (See 1 John 4:1–3.)

When this prophet came up on the platform to preach, he looked at my son and said, "Young man, you have a learning disability. Can I pray for you?" He then pointed to Elias and said, "This is your son! Come up here!" Next, he turned to his left and pointed to me saying, "Come up here! All three of you are a family!" He told us to join hands. Then he told us about our life and how Satan had conspired against our home from the moment Ricky was conceived. He described all that had been happening to us, repeated that we had been in eight wrecks and even described the alarm clock going off every thirty minutes for the first six years of Ricky's life.

He continued to exhort us with several other words from the Lord for all of us. There were eleven points in all: 1) Ricky is ordained of God; 2) he is consecrated and dedicated unto God; 3) he is terribly retarded with no hope, except from the Lord; 4) he will be in the world but not of it; 5) the Lord will heal him very shortly so that He can use him for an End-Time harvest; 6) God Himself will educate Ricky; 7) God had brought us out of our church because He did not want Ricky to be contaminated by tradition; 8) God would not allow Ricky to be taught by traditional methods and strategies; 9) God would allow Ricky to go to college, but Ricky would end up teaching there; 10) Ricky would learn the Bible from the ancient languages and from the history of the ancient church; 11) Ricky would turn the church world upside down.

I am so glad that I didn't have to unlearn erroneous doctrine about the prophetic word. Many believe that prophecy is universal and is only given to a whole nation or a whole congregation rather than to an individual. What good is the prophetic word for edification if it is only universal? What does the saint do when he is crying out for God to give him some direction and the church says there is no specific word for him? There are many instances in the Bible where prophetic words were not given to a nation, but to an individual person. Ahab, David and Paul are just a few examples among many others. (See 1 Kings 21:11–22:53; Jeremiah 11:21; 14:14; Ezekiel 29:2; 37:2; 38:2; 1 Samuel 9:1–27; 2 Chronicles 15:3; Nehemiah 6:12; Proverbs 30:1; 31:1; 2 Chronicles 18:7; 20:37; John 11:51; Isaiah 7:14; Jude 14; 1 Kings 1; 11:29–43; 13:18–20; 14:2; 16:7; Acts 21:1–13; 2 Samuel 7:8–17; 12:1–8.)

It was Billy Jo Fain who gave prophetic words that were directed to this family. He spoke mighty words about our family's part in the End-Time harvest and about our ministry being based in Jacksonville. After receiving several prophetic words that morning, my husband cried out to God and asked, "Why? Why? Why? Why were we chosen to receive the promise and the blessings?" At the revival the next morning, the prophet called him out and answered his question. "It is not you. It is God's sovereignty and especially His grace!"

I had the vision of the wheel angel a little more than three weeks before this experience. This man was the first prophet that I had seen and his prophetic word was the first that I had ever heard. Since prophecy was new to me, I could do nothing but believe. I had nothing else to hold on to except the prophecy and the vision that God had given. This prophecy confirmed that vision. Both of these were like an immovable log in the midst of a mighty river that provided a secure place for a drowning victim to hold. That's just what I did. I held on tightly to the vision and the prophecy. It saved me from drowning in a river of hopelessness. I am very glad that Billy Jo Fain lived long enough to see God heal and educate Ricky.

During this same time, the tent revival gave birth to other revivals in Jacksonville and Fernandina. This great tent revival is where Ricky experienced the baptism of the Holy Spirit and heard the voice of God speak to him audibly. Billy Jo Fain told Ricky that God wanted to speak to him as a friend talks to another friend, face-to-face. After hearing this, Ricky went home, went to bed and waited. Finally God was able to break through the demonic barrier that had tried to prevent Ricky from hearing God. For that next twenty-four hour period, Ricky heard the audible voice of God. His room was so filled with God's glory, that smoke visibly filled the room. God spoke many things to him that night. This was not the last time that Ricky was granted the privilege of hearing the audible voice of God for twenty-four hours.

After this, Ricky was given his first vision. He saw heaven open and the hands of God coming down and breaking through the dark clouds. Underneath the hands the words were written, "For I shall bring forth truth out of darkness for the sake of my people." The Lord told him that this would be the logo for his ministry.

Several other manifestations of the Lord happened to others during this time. The first manifestation was a blue mist. It covered the tent visibly, flowing around and touching my sister Sue three separate times. As the mist passed over the heads of the people, many fell out as if they were dead.

The second manifestation happened to a coworker of mine when she attended the revival. Though she had never gone to a Pentecostal revival, she would never forget this one. She accepted the Lord as her Savior and experienced one of the most severe cases of being "drunk in the Spirit" that I have ever seen in my life. She stayed this way for five straight days. At work I saw her stagger from one side of the hall to the other saying, "Be not drunk with wine but with the Spirit saith the Lord!" (See Ephesians 5:18.) Needless to say, I was begging God to lift the Spirit from her. So many people from all over the mill were coming to see what was going on that my boss asked me to lift whatever was on her. I replied that if this was of God, everything would work out and no one would be harmed. Her testimony resulted in much repentance and deliverance at work.

The third manifestation was the visible sighting of an angel. One night a man appeared in front of the tent. He spoke with such wisdom and had such a holy appearance that there was no question that he was an angel. His appearance was absolutely beautiful. Why did he come? I had been studying the demonic even though I was not yet mature enough to handle the topic of demons. When a saint studies demons, evil spirits will congregate around. Therefore, the saint had better know how to fight them. The first thing that I told the angel was that I was studying demons. He replied, "Why study demons? Study angels! They help the saints." I was dumbfounded. I had thought that studying demons was a mark of maturity. I learned so much from our conversation. The last thing I asked was, "Can we pray for you?" He humbly bowed his head and accepted our prayer. Since then, this same man has appeared in two visions, proclaiming himself as an angel of the Lord and coming in the name of the Lord. From our conversation, I found out that he believed that Jesus Christ was born from a virgin, was crucified and arose from the grave. He also proclaimed that Jesus Christ is God, and he accepted all the fundamental doctrines of Christianity. Remember Hebrews 13:2: "Be not forgetful to entertain strangers: for thereby some have entertained angels unawares."

Elias also had two notable experiences with the Lord. The first can only be described as amazing. It was not a vision or a dream, but what can only be called a "translation" or "a rapture." In this, a person is either caught up bodily as were Enoch, Elijah and Philip or his soul is caught up without the body. (See Genesis 5:24; 2 Kings 2:9–12; Acts 8:39.)

Elias' soul was not caught up to heaven, but to the valley near the mountain where the body of Moses was buried. As he turned and looked, numerous people were sitting down in countless ranks doing nothing at all. He saw only a few workers running up the mountain and back down to the valley, gathering the gifts and the blessings that God has for all saints. A mighty angel appeared at the top of the mountain. When the feet of this angel landed upon the mountain, blue sparks went everywhere and illuminated the land and the sky. His appearance was so bright with light and glory that nothing on this earth can describe it. This brightness spread forth from the mountain down to the valley. Elias had never seen such a beautiful creature. Words cannot truly describe angels.

Though Elias was far away, the angel said to him audibly, "Come!" Elias got up from where he was sitting and began to walk toward the angel. The angel said, "No," and pointed his finger while Elias continued to float toward him. Finally, Elias reached the angel who, by his power, set him down. At that point the angel said, "All those people who were shown to be doing nothing for the sake of Christ have been sitting right in the place where they were saved. They have not moved an inch. If these people are not extremely careful, they will be sitting right there when Jesus comes! All the gifts and blessings for my people are found up here upon this mountain if they will come!" This profound statement still echoes in our minds. We have never forgotten these words. It has motivated us to continually strive to answer His call.

Before this translation ended, the angel showed Elias that Ricky was upon the mountain where the gifts and blessings were, receiving a hedge of protection around him. All of us had prayed all week before this experience that God would do just that.

Symbolically, the mountain is heaven and the valley is the earth. The few coming up and down are those who, through prayers and beseeching God, have entered heaven and received the gifts and blessings of the Lord.

The second and last experience during this time happened when Elias was coming home from shopping. He drove down Broward Road as he often did with nothing appearing out of the ordinary. As he approached our home, he stopped behind a car. Instead of going around it, he sat waiting. The Lord spoke audibly and suddenly, "Look up!" He looked up and saw a speeding car traveling at sixty-five miles per hour behind him. He had only enough time to say, "Jesus help me!" before his car was hit. As he said those words, a blue mist entered his car and surrounded him. The mist was visible and tangible. Elias got out of the vehicle and said, "Well, Lord, it is yours if you want Satan to tear it up!" A police officer heard what he said and thought he was in shock. A friend, who happened to be present, said to the police officer, "He's all right. He is a praying man and believes that the Lord has preserved him through this." That's exactly what God did! The car was totaled, but Elias was fine.

Ricky was fourteen years old when this prophecy was given. Having received this assurance, I became bold in the Lord. I went everywhere telling everyone that God was going to heal my son. People looked at me strangely. They thought that I was crazy and pitied me. Many laughed at me during the two-year time period before Ricky's miracle. Even my family did not understand what was going on. One of my sisters called after Ricky had graduated from college, crying and asking forgiveness. She could not understand with her finite mind what a marvelous and mighty miracle God had wrought within our family.

Too often we seek and beg God for miracles and then, when they come to our families, we reject them or deny that they ever came at all. Only by the grace of God does He still perform miracles, even in the midst of our denial and rejections. Thank God for His grace!

CHAPTER 5

Aftermath of a Miracle

Between 1975 and December of 1977, Elias and I continued to have Ricky tutored every Saturday, even during the summer. Even though we had received God's promise, we did not stand idly by doing nothing. We kept holding on to that promise! It was all that we had. There were very few signs that God was working to fulfill His words to us about Ricky. Yet, He was working behind the scenes, placing pieces of the puzzle together. He showed His true mastery and handiwork, demonstrating that He is truly the Great Architect.

In December of 1977, the life of Ricky was instantaneously and totally changed. The three of us went to a Full Gospel revival at another church. The preacher, Al Edenfield, sang and sang. As he was singing, he went back to where Ricky was sitting and said, "Young man, you have a learning disability! Can I pray for you?" Ricky replied yes.

The preacher put his hand on the head of Ricky then snatched it back saying, "The Lord has heard your cries as you lay awake at night saying, 'Why can't I learn like other children?' If your mother will stand on faith and put you in the tenth grade, God will fill in the foundation!" These words so struck me that I became paralyzed all over. I could not think or realize what God had just done. Words cannot describe the state in which I found myself. However, thank God, the preacher knew that I did not understand or fully realize what had happened to my son that very night and instant! As I was going out the door he said, "Little sister, you did not understand what happened to your son! The Lord said that He has healed your son! In three days, University Christian School will call you to take him out of that school. The teachers cannot help him and are using him as a babysitter in his class." I knew that this was true because a teacher had told me this. I did not become excited over what the preacher had said because I was in shock.

I continued to feel as if I was in a fog until the school called me three days later. The elementary principal, Mrs. Sanders, was on the phone. She said that I screamed out to her, "Mrs. Sanders, the Lord has healed my boy! Put him in the tenth grade! I will be over there in a few minutes!" Although the school was thirty minutes away, I flew there, breaking the speed limit. I ran into the school yelling out loudly, "God has healed my son!" Can you imagine what Mrs. Sanders was thinking? She thought that I had lost it and was having a nervous breakdown over my son. She sent me to the head principal of the school who was her husband. I told him the same thing that I had said to her. Of course, at first he did not believe that God had healed my son. He said, "Mrs. Roberts, you are going to destroy your son!

Jumping seven grades is impossible for anyone! This school has done all that it can do!" Then I noticed a Bible verse on the wall. It read, "But Jesus beheld them, and said unto them, With men this is impossible; but with God all things are possible (Matthew 19:26)." I told him very kindly, but with holy boldness, "Mr. Sanders, if you don't believe that my son fits in that verse, take it down because you are a hypocrite!" Mr. Sanders wanted me to send Ricky to a psychologist named Dr. Smith to have him analyzed. I said, "There is no problem with this. I have had Ricky analyzed by so many psychologists and psychiatrists that another doesn't bother me." When I told him to call his doctor, he then made an appointment.

When I saw Dr. Smith, the very first thing I told him was that God had healed Ricky. Dr. Smith said to me, "I do not believe in that junk!" The doctor had already been informed about Ricky and his learning disability. I said to him, "I am a believer and God's work can be tested! I want you to test God's work, whatever the cost!"

A few days later, Mrs. Dugger and I went for a consultation on the test results. Dr. Smith said, "I don't know what to tell you people! Put this boy in the tenth grade by all means! He was doing algebra, trigonometry and all other tenth grade work that he had never had!"

The Sanders did not want to place Ricky in the tenth grade unless it was agreed that he would remain on trial there for the rest of the school year until it could be verified that he could really do the work. They knew that on or before December of 1977, Ricky had only been working at a third-grade level. Between Christmas vacation and the beginning of the next semester, Ricky prepared himself to enter the tenth grade. His special education class remained his homeroom. It was a life or death matter for Ricky. His whole future hung in the balance. It was time for God's work to be truly tested!

Although God had miraculously worked in Ricky, the teachers did not want a retarded student in their classes, even on trial. They could not comprehend that God had healed my son and still labeled Ricky retarded. This was a terrible problem for Ricky, but it was no problem for God. Several months before God healed Ricky, a teacher named Mr. Hazlett moved from Pennsylvania to be a history teacher at the school. He agreed to have a retarded child in his class since he himself was the father of a child with a handicap. Elias and I saw God's hand in working out these details. Each special education teacher also had a part in this miracle and played valuable roles in God's workings.

After nine weeks on trial, Mr. Hazlett called me to talk. He said, "The first Monday morning after the Christmas vacation Ricky came into my classroom. The other students, knowing that he was retarded, began to laugh at him. His face and eyes were downcast and he began to tremble. I put him in the front of the classroom where he took out his notebook and began to write down everything that I wrote on the blackboard. I went very slowly in explaining the lesson. That first week there was a test on the subject material and Ricky scored one hundred. In six weeks he was tutoring many of the other students who had made fun of him."

During this probationary period, other teachers also decided to allow Ricky in their classrooms after Mr. Hazlett's experience. They all had to hand in regular reports, in addition to his report card, on his progress. At the end of the first nine weeks, Mrs. Sanders called me crying and said, "I think you need to read the reports of the teachers!" As I drove up to the school, Mrs. Sanders met me with a smile on her face. She gave me a teacher's report that read, "Mrs. Sanders, this report concerns Ricky Roberts who has a ninety-six average in my class. He is a well-behaved young man. Do you have any more special education students like Ricky? Please send them to my class!" In that half of the year, Ricky not only learned how to diagram sentences, but made the honor roll as well.

I will never forget another day that Mrs. Sanders called me excited about Ricky. All the time that he was in the special education class she had never heard him laugh. That day she had heard him laugh out loud for the first time. She said that she felt like Ricky had discovered a long lost continent.

It is impossible to explain the joy Elias and I felt when we came home from work and found Ricky doing his homework. He was never as happy as when he turned sixteen, knowing that Jesus healed him.

When the school year ended, I went to Mrs. Sanders and asked for their best English teacher to tutor Ricky over the summer. She said that she would trust Ricky with only one teacher, Mrs. Glidden. She had taught college and also worked for a book company as their main editor. I knew that she was the person that we needed to work with him. That summer she tutored Ricky five times. During four of these times she taught four different levels of English to him: elementary, junior high school, high school, and two years of college. The fifth time she spent two hours testing him to see whether he had learned it. She came through the living room with her hands in the air praising Jesus about what He had done for Ricky.

Ricky entered the tenth grade for credit in the 1978–79 school year. The teachers were strictly grading him, making sure that they all had the same high standards for him. They wanted to make sure that he was truly earning his grades.

The very first day Ricky was called into the principal's office and told that he would have to take U.S. history for tenth-grade credit. Miss Cover, who taught this subject, was extremely hard. No one had ever made a grade higher than a C in her class. She planned on going to graduate school to be a lawyer. Ricky told the principal, "God has not healed me to run from anyone! Give her to me!"

I overheard Ricky on the phone one day talking to Miss Cover about his report card. He said, "Miss Cover, I have averaged my grade and I have a B! My report card said that I had a C." Miss Cover acknowledged her mistake and changed his grade the next day. Ricky kept on working until he made two A's in her class.

Finding Ricky on his knees early in the morning was still very common. He often prayed himself to sleep. Sometimes his legs would be asleep, and we would have to help him into bed. While God gave Ricky the ability to learn, He also demanded that he study. Ricky applied himself to his academic subjects relentlessly. It was as if he had an unquenchable thirst for knowledge that continues to this day.

That year, he was nominated for membership in the National Honor Society. He passed the entire year with four A's and four B's. Elias and I received that report card with an unspeakable joy. For so many years, Satan had worked to prevent Ricky from learning, but God made it possible. I thank God we believed Him and not Satan!

In the summer Ricky began to teach himself about computers. This was a skill he would need very badly later on as God walked our family through what He wanted for our lives.

In the eleventh grade, Ricky was initiated into the National Honor Society with a beautiful candlelight service. Mrs. Bishop, the sponsor, said that night, "Lord, I am thankful for my son, but no one could be as thankful as the parents of Ricky are!"

For the first time in his life, Ricky could hold his head up high with joy on his face. Satan had lied to Ricky for all those years, but God continued to speak the truth. In the eleventh grade Ricky averaged seven A's and one B.

In the twelfth grade, he took business law as a subject. The teacher, Mrs. Richardson, had been a substitute teacher in his special education class a few years before God had healed Ricky. She couldn't remember if she had ever taught him before at University Christian School. Ricky reminded her of the class he had been in. As she recalled this she was dumbfounded. Her only memory of Ricky in that class was his struggle to pronounce the word "and." Now, he was taking business law, pronouncing twelfth-grade words and defining them.

As a senior, he also studied "Old English" as part of a literature class. I could not understand why God would want Ricky to take this. I now know what God's sovereign purpose was in having him do this. Most of the books that we have bought are written in an ancient English style that Ricky can understand!

In 1981, Ricky received the International Youth in Achievement of the World award. Only ten thousand teenagers are inducted annually. Again in 1982, during his first year of college, he received the same award.

The night Ricky graduated from high school he received every award but two. When he went up to receive his first award, the principal told Ricky, "Just stay up here, you will walk yourself to death!" He earned the highest grade average ever achieved in business law, was Class Honor Student and Best Student in Religion. Elias and I had prayed that Jesus would receive glory and honor. That night Ricky also received the Outstanding Award. The principal asked, "Why is Ricky receiving the Outstanding Award? I don't think that he will mind if I tell you that when he came to this school he was mentally retarded and in our special education class for about five years. Ricky told me that as his faith in the Lord Jesus Christ grew, his learning disability was healed! It does appear that this is true since he jumped seven grades, impossibility without God stepping into the situation!" After the graduation ceremony people gathered around Ricky wanting to know what had happened. The Lord received the entire honor and glory that night because of His grace in Ricky's life.

After the graduation ceremony, the Lord spoke to Ricky saying, "I have taken you from the tail and made you the head. Now, Ricky, I want you to go on a fast!" This was a difficult time to go without food because we had a garden and were harvesting our fresh vegetables. At first, Elias and I did not know how long the fast would be. After twenty-one days had passed, we became upset. We began to cry and pray that God would help Ricky. Elias would push his plate of food away and cry out to God to allow him to do the fasting for Ricky. Ricky fasted for forty days without anything to eat, drinking only water. What was so amazing about this fast was that one day before the end of this fast, God told Ricky that since he was obedient, he could eat anything immediately after the fast was over and it would not hurt him in the least. Ricky told his father and me what God had said. Ricky wanted to eat a steak, French fries, salad, and bread and drink tea. Elias and I knew that eating so much was not recommended after a long fast, but we obeyed the voice of God and cooked Ricky all that he had asked. When the fast was over, Ricky sat down and ate all that we had prepared for him, suffering no harm. Obedience is truly better than sacrifice.

When Ricky began to go to college, he attended a junior college here in Jacksonville. I told the counselor about what God had done in the healing of my son. She said meanly, "He will earn his grades here!" I responded, "He had better earn it! At that high school, I paid for his education and it was not given to him in the least!" When he was tested, he placed in the second year of college. He went there until the middle of his second year.

Before he finished, the Lord spoke to him and said, "Come out of that college because you have learned all that I want you to know there. Your mother is not going to like this, but I want you to study the Bible and the books that I tell you to buy." What God wanted was truly a shock! I thought that Ricky would get a degree in computer science, but the Father had other plans for him. I was not going to get between God and my son. That would have been dangerous. I told him to go and buy the books that God led him to buy. In about an hour, he came out with a list of books. I turned off dinner, and we went to a Baptist bookstore. The manager had never heard of these books.

Again, we found ourselves praying and crying to God. I asked God if we were descending into fanaticism. We went to other bookstores where the managers also had never heard of these books. All the way to work I could do nothing but cry and pray to God again. The next day the Lord led me to call a church in Oklahoma. At first, I found no help, but God said to me, "Try again!" This time I got through and told the woman on the telephone the story about God healing my son. She gave me the name of a man whose professional name was "the Book Finder." I called him and he not only knew about the books, but also agreed to help Ricky find them. God helped us find all the books, and we then bought them. Later God opened other doors and means by which Ricky could find other books. Right before my eyes the prophecy given when Ricky was fourteen years old was being fulfilled.

During this time, I would come home from work and find Ricky reading with twenty or twenty-five books on the living room floor around him. He could summarize each page and remember what subject had been discussed on a certain page. It was common for Ricky to come into our bedroom at about three or four in the morning to wake us up and tell us what he had found out from his studies.

The Lord did not always make it easy on us to find the book that he would tell Ricky to buy. Once the Lord told him to buy a book, and we tried everywhere but could not find it. Ricky began to cry and pray to God. He told the Lord, "My father and mother will buy the book if we can find it. Help us." The Lord said, "Ricky, tell your mother to quit fretting! Call the Library of Congress and have them reprint it!" The Library of Congress made a loose-leaf copy for us, which we had permanently bound.

One night after about five years of studying the books that God told him to buy, Ricky was praying around midnight.

He cried out to the Lord because he felt led to get a doctorate but knew that no college would accept his unorthodox education. The Lord responded to him by saying, "Render therefore unto Caesar things which are Caesar's, and unto God the things that are God's." Ricky said, "Father, are You telling me that I can go to college?" The Lord said yes to his desire and not long afterward showed him a college in North Carolina that would take him.

When Ricky started at that College, the president gave him a year of college free if he would do research for them. Ricky agreed. The officers of that college said that they did not teach Ricky; he taught the college. Remember the prophecy!

Ricky earned several doctorates, and a Ph.D. in Old Testament and New Testament studies. He graduated summa cum laude and was the first student to graduate at that college with a 4.00 GPA. Between 1982 and 2003, Ricky received numerous other awards, such as Community Leaders of America (1983), Young Personalities of the South (1983), Young Personalities of America (1983), Biographical Roll of Honor (1984), International Book of Honor (1985), Who's Who in America (1998), 1,000 Great Americans (2002) and Who's Who in the World (2000–2003).

I have been asked so many times what I would have done with my son if God had not healed him. That is a place I do not want to go. I see nothing but grace in the miracle wrought for my son. That grace can come upon anyone if he or she will meet God halfway. That is all that God ever requires. When I do ponder that question, there is absolutely no regret over his life. His father and I treasured him and were proud of him even before God healed him. We believe that God gives only the best gifts to His children. Satan is the one who damages and destroys, tempting us into the consequences of rebellion.

When asked to describe this miracle of God healing his mind, Ricky replies, "It is like living in a very dark tunnel for years. Then, suddenly, a match is lit. The small light from this match becomes brighter and brighter until finally the light engulfs the whole tunnel." In his life, all of this was done in an instant, through the power of God working internally upon his brain. Not until Dr. Smith tested Ricky did we have any proof that God had done anything. Still, Elias, Ricky, and I held on!

Time and again, Ricky has flashbacks about his sixteen years of retardation. A certain smell, image, taste, touch or sound can bring all of those memories back in a flood. God desires that Ricky will never forget his state of retardation. For years Ricky has suffered from a recurring nightmare. He finds himself sitting in a high school classroom, unable to read a word, failing an important test and not graduating. Only when Ricky wakes up, does he realize that it was only a dream. Around the year 2000 this nightmare finally disappeared when Ricky took authority over it. Satan used this dream to torment my son. Thank God the saints have the victory and power over Satan through the blood of Christ in every realm.

Even before Ricky's healing and nine years of higher education, he was enrolled in the school of the Spirit, learning from the Holy Spirit about the spiritual gifts and how they must be used. From this age to the present, Ricky has been used greatly in the prophetic ministry, giving words of edification and comfort to the brokenhearted. God works gifts of healing and miracles through him as well. Ricky, in his state of retardation, could not reach up to God, but God could reach down to him, using the gifts of the Holy Spirit through him.

Since 1975, the Lord has granted Ricky many supernatural experiences. Besides hearing the audible voice of God two notable times, Ricky has visibly seen the wings of angels flying across his room. He has seen the glory of God in such intensity that it lit up his whole room and almost blinded him for a time. He has heard heavenly sounds that cannot be described or uttered by a human voice. He has smelled the sweet odors of heaven enter his room and the hellish odors of demons as well. He has had countless visions that include the Lord, angels and demons, among other things. In visions, my son has seen heaven and hell, and even the very throne room of God.

Ricky and I may chronicle these visions and other experiences in a later book. The most vivid time we'll recount is during a twenty-two day fast when the very presence of hell entered his room for eight of those days. I will never forget it!

Our family is so grateful to God for bringing us through the waters of suffering to walk on dry land. What we know of God's power and might could never have been learned by us taking the easy way. We praise Him for giving us His strength and the courage to hold on to His word and promises until they were fulfilled. To Him be all glory and honor forever!

CHAPTER 6

Testimonies and Proofs of a Miracle

A Statement From a Thankful Mother
By Dorothy Roberts

I am just a country mother who loves her family and had only a simple and uneducated faith. I knew only enough to believe what I read in the Bible. No preacher, teacher, theologian or any other scholar could take the words of life from my hands and from my life when it came down to my son.

I can say that all that I knew about prayer was to end it in the name of Jesus. What I learned about intercession came from none but the Holy Spirit. It was He who led me all the way and upon whom I rested my faith and my case.

The parts of this book written by me contain my thoughts in my own style. The style is like me, simple and straightforward. By staying true to myself, I pray that this style will touch the heart of those in a state of hopelessness.

I encourage all seekers of truth and all who feel hopeless to reach out to God for the answer, to step out into the deep waters of our faith, to lay down tradition and listen to God rather than man. What God did for my family, He is well able to do for all!

A Statement From a Pastor by Jeana Tomlinson, Co-Pastor, New Covenant Ministries of Jacksonville, Florida

When I first met Dot Roberts, she did not know who I was. She was testifying to my son about the good things that God had done for her own son, Ricky. Tears streamed down her face as she recalled all the years that she had interceded for a miracle of God for her boy. I was so captivated by her sincerity that I listened intently for the duration of her testimony. I stood spellbound by her account of the three years of desperate weeping, which preceded one of the greatest miracles I have ever heard. Then, I assured her that I indeed felt that God had brought us together. She spoke as a modern-day Hannah, weeping centuries ago for a son that she could give back to God. In her desperation, God came through and granted her the desire of her heart.

My desire is that you will be as blessed as I am by the mighty deeds done in the mind and heart of Dr. Ricky. You will be particularly impressed at the significant role his mother, Dot, has played in the final orchestration of one of the most spectacular signs and wonders of our day.

Does God still heal? Yes!

Will He do it for you? Absolutely!

Read and study this account and permit the God of the miraculous to move in your life. Learn from Dot's walk through tears how to summon the Sovereign. Jesus Christ the same yesterday, and today, and forever (Hebrews 13:8).

MEMORIES OF A TEACHER
BY SALLY YOUNG

I first met Ricky at University Christian School in Jacksonville, Florida, in 1973. I was the Special Education teacher there and taught both the mentally handicapped as well as those who were significantly behind in their academics. At the time, Ricky was coming to our school from a regular sixth grade class in the public schools. I tested him, and he was only reading on a primer level, which is well below first grade.

Ricky was very sweet natured, wanted to learn and had a desire to serve God. He loved the Lord. I remember one time I asked the students to give sacrificially to some missionaries, and we had a little box to put their offerings in. Everyone gave a little, but I remember Ricky gave all that he had. He was always that way. He was always loving, giving and caring. You could tell how much God was already working in his heart even at that young age.

I had Ricky in my class that year and the next. We labored every day on reading, language and math skills. I knew I could help him, but I did not think he would ever catch up to his grade level. His mother would even bring him over to my house to be privately tutored in reading because she wanted to help him to learn to read and to become independent.

It was to be many years later that Ricky and his mother shared with me that he not only caught up to his peers but also far exceeded them and myself in his education and college career. It was obvious that I had been part of the miracle of healing. Was I responsible? No, God had his hand on Ricky all along. In His plan, Ricky had to be far behind in his academics for God to work. If he had only been a year or two behind, people would not have recognized the miracle that God performed. In John 9:1–3, Jesus' disciples saw a man who had been blind from birth and asked Jesus who sinned that he had been born blind. Jesus answered that this happened so that the work of God might be displayed in his life. That is exactly what God did in Ricky's life. God is being glorified through this, not only in healing Ricky, but also by using him to teach and help others.

I am privileged to have taught Ricky and to have known the loving spirit of Jesus manifested in Ricky. But most of all, I glorify and praise Jesus for His mighty work. Our class Bible verse was Philippians 4:13, "I can do all things through Christ which strengtheneth me." Ricky proved that to be true! Praise the Lord!

Memories of a Neighbor
By Virginia Harrell

I was a neighbor of Elias, Dot and Ricky Roberts. Ricky was born with severe learning disabilities. Ricky's private school kindergarten principal had recommended that he repeat kindergarten, but he went on to first grade, which he had to repeat. I had given Ricky's mother some word and math tutoring cards, but they did not seem to help very much.

In 1970 I was a substitute teacher in a public school third grade classroom in which Ricky was a student. When I asked the class to please stand and repeat the pledge of allegiance to our flag, everyone in the class stood except Ricky. I had to say, "Ricky, you have to stand and say the pledge of allegiance." Finally, he stood up and went through the motions of the pledge of allegiance with the class. Evidently, his teachers had not pushed him to take part in class exercises, math or reading. Shortly afterward, I told his mother that she really should send him to the University Christian School's special education class.

Years later when Ricky was sixteen, he came to my house to read for me out of a sixth grade reading book. I did not think he would be able to read very much of the page, but I was amazed to hear him read the words and to attack the really difficult words in the proper manner. This was truly a miracle. I remember this vividly because I did not think he would ever be able to accomplish even this small feat.

Memories of Mrs. Bruce Dugger

I taught a multi-age special education class at University Christian School in the school year of 1977–1978. One of my students, Ricky Roberts, was a sixteen-year-old boy reading on a third grade level at that time. Most of the students had been in this class together for several years. They were like a family to one another in the midst of a world that was unkind to them. Ricky was very happy to spend a good part of his days helping the younger children learn.

I felt a heavy responsibility to teach and push Ricky to climb to higher levels. I began trying to push his reading, math and language forward. Before Christmas, I agreed with others to have him professionally tested to see what potential he could actually achieve.

His mom, Ricky and I visited Dr. Smith after the results were gathered to make an academic plan. Dr. Smith encouraged the school to let me put Ricky into some sophomore classes to see how he could cope. He was placed in world history and other subjects along with his special education class. I continued working with him on his reading, language and math skills.

Ricky did very well, and the following year he was promoted out of special education and placed in sophomore classes for credit. A lot of hard work and great perseverance found Ricky graduating with honors a few years later.

Yet I must admit, it was not Ricky alone that accomplished all of this. Ricky, as he was, could not have been able to achieve any or all of this. I beheld the visible and inner workings of God firsthand! I never will forget it as long as I live.

Memories of a Principal
By Margaret J. Glidden

Ricky Roberts (of Jacksonville, Florida) graduated from University Christian School after attending for eight years. This young man came to the school as a nonreader with learning disabilities of a severe nature. Because he scored several grades below the classmates of his age, he was placed in a special education class when he entered the school. Although he was twelve years old and in the sixth grade, he was reading below kindergarten level. Ricky continued to work in a small, ungraded class under the direction of a special education teacher for about five years. Things appeared hopeless for Ricky, but his trust in God grew. He could not visualize graduation ahead for him and the thought of having a diploma was remote. He had resigned himself to moving along without the success that others always appeared to get. He said, "I cried to God to learn, and He taught me!"

In the winter of 1977, something out of the ordinary happened to Ricky. In December, God (at church) moved upon Ricky by His supernatural power through a preacher's laying hands upon him. He was completely and immediately healed of all his learning disabilities. Instantaneously, God filled in seven years of school (from the third grade to the tenth grade). The improvement was not due to anything that man did, but God, improving Ricky's mental capacities. At the age of sixteen, God could completely and utterly finish what He had started. If God had filled all the levels at one time, Ricky's brain would not have been able to sustain it.

Memories of Robin Schottleutner

In 1974 my husband and I took our first teaching jobs at University Christian School. I was to fill the vacancy left by the previous special education teacher, Sally Young. She had developed the program from its beginning, and since I was inexperienced, I simply tried to pick up and continue where she left off.

When I think back on that classroom of children, ages ranging from six years to sixteen years of age, I remember Ricky as a big boy sitting at his desk doing seat work with all the concentration and effort that he could muster. Though our classroom was air conditioned, he would perspire as if the calculations of his math problems were a mile run. Scholastically, he was behind his age. The reading and math problems took him long periods of time to complete. At various times, there were students Ricky's age that showed anger or embarrassment at being in the special education class.

As he progressed in school, I'm sure many noticed the growing confidence he possessed. One of the last phone conversations I had with him before we moved away showed me of his widening interests and his ability to give advice. He asked me if I had a garden, and I told him I was enjoying growing flowers. "Well," he said, "you ought to have a vegetable garden because you can eat the vegetables, but you can't eat your flowers." Though I continue to spend my time with flowers in the yard, Ricky's words still ring true.

There have been many occasions when my husband and I have spoken of Ricky's desire and determination to succeed in school. It brought us great joy to hear of his uncommon achievements and to know he has given the glory to God. Mrs. Roberts once asked me if I believed God could still heal. As I look back on her question, I realize she knew the answer to Ricky's needs rested in God's power and ability, not in the efforts of a teacher or in her son's desire to learn.

CHAPTER 7

Personal Evidence of a Miracle

Dr. Margaret Glidden's Responses to a Negative Article Written about Ricky Roberts

The article entitled "The Mysterious Metamorphosis of Ricky Roberts" that appeared in the Jacksonville Times-Union on Sunday, April 16, 2006, was not mysterious as the title would indicate. I would call it a miracle. Furthermore, it was not a metamorphosis, but a miraculous, instantaneous healing by the power of the Holy Spirit.

The reporter interviewed me before this article went to print. If he had included all the information I gave him regarding Dr. Roberts when he was a youth at University Christian School while I was the principal of that institution, he would not have been able to draw his readers to a conclusion which would leave a question in their minds as to whether this youth reached the amazing goals he reached by "pushing himself and trying hard" or whether it was a total transformation which changed his ability to learn in an instant. I gave the reporter specific instances which proved that he was not just changed—but transformed in his thinking ability.

When I read the article, which included statements that I consider rude and uncalled for (i.e. his pronunciation of a word, and "massive tinted glasses"), it was written as by one who was trying to reach everybody—those who believed that God was still performing miracles, and those who had no faith at all and would probably see Roberts as a phony. He was apparently trying to reach all readers. This reminds me of the man we heard about who wore a Union shirt and Confederate pants during the Civil War in order to get through unscathed. However, this man wound up getting shot at by both sides. This writer, too, is experiencing a similar attack.

The reporter spent a great deal of time attempting to interpret "100 pages of his academic records from University Christian and Duval County public school system" in order to disregard the obvious truth that by meeting and visiting with Roberts, it could not be denied that he was no longer retarded, but rather an educated, brilliant, and articulate teacher. The reporter used educational records that he had never been trained to interpret—throwing out scores and comments about them that he was not prepared to understand. Dr. Roberts does not need anyone to prove that an unexplainable experience occurred in his life.

However, here is my conclusion based upon the facts in a more orderly and direct manner. And other educators did help in this analysis, for which I am gratefully thankful!

What do the educational and medical records say about Ricky Roberts?

Overall, the educational records show that Ricky was mentally retarded or challenged and behind his grade level. He stayed in a special education setting for approximately five years, moved from that setting to a mainstream class equaling his normal school grade level (tenth grade), succeeded in graduating high school, and won high honors. Further, the records show a great metamorphosis had taken place. The records show that he advanced from third grade to tenth grade instantaneously. This speaks for itself. Nothing but a miracle can explain it.

The records are educational records and cannot be correctly interpreted by unprofessional or uneducated persons who have never been trained to interpret these kinds of records. At over 100 pages, it takes much time to study all the records to obtain a truthful interpretation. The interpretation here given is not Dr. Roberts', but is the interpretation of educators and counselors who were consulted for their educational opinion. Further, those consulted also gave their opinions about other educational subjects.

The Teachers Speak Out

In 1969 Mrs. Durden, Ricky's first grade teacher, said: "Ricky gets along well with his peers. He has much difficulty with letters and sounds."

In 1969–70 Mrs. Jordan, Ricky's second grade teacher, wrote: "Mother plans to take him to Gainesville Clinic for checkout in the summer of 1971."

In 1970–71 Mrs. Grisson, Ricky's third grade teacher, said: "Seems to have a block against reading."

In 1971–72 Mrs. Hedgeeoth said, "His reading is very difficult."

In 1972–73 Mrs. White said: "Ricky is very low in all areas."

In 1973–74, special education teacher Mrs. Young wrote: "Ricky works very hard but is far behind grade level. He may need special education throughout his schooling. Reading is his weakest subject." In another place, she writes: "Ricky was promoted year after year to sixth grade when he reads only on a primer level! He came into special education with no reading ability at all."

In 1974–75, special education teacher Mrs. Schottleutner wrote: "Ricky has done a good job this year. He tries at every task. At times he acts childlike. Reading continues to be very weak."

After Ricky's healing, in 1977–78, Mrs. Dugger, stated: "Ricky has worked extremely hard to pull himself up. He has taken math, history and Bible in high school (upper level) and has done well. He should progress well completely in the secondary level."

Records Examined

One part of the records show that Ricky scored in public school far below average in the first, second, third, fourth, fifth, and sixth grades.

Records from the Duval County School Board all show that Ricky was below average intelligence. Every record states, "Below grade level." This is confirmed over and over again.

In 1972, Ricky was given Comprehensive Tests of Basic Skills from Duval County. All these tests show that he was very low in all areas. This agrees with what Mrs. White said.

In his possession, Ricky has the records from Shands Hospital showing that he was a medical patient there. These records show that his IQ was extremely low.

The records show that in 1970 he was enrolled in the Reading Research Foundation. Their conclusion was that his IQ was extremely low.

The records show that Ricky was in special education from 1973 to 1977 respectively. Counting 1973 as the first year, he was there approximately five years. They show that a great change took place for him to be in special education for these years and then jump to the tenth grade level. No other student has ever done this. His 1975 and 1976 records show some improvement.

The SAT tests used during his time in special education followed this format: The teacher would read the instructions to the students and then leave the students to read and work on their own. Many students who were in special education were not able to read, or could not read enough to understand the questions. Ricky was a non-reader for a considerable part of those five years, and then began to be able to read due to God working upon his mind. Mrs. Dugger said that the SAT scores for all the students cannot be recognized as official because of this format. For example, in several places, students including Ricky marked two or more answers. This shows that he could not read the questions, and by this he could not answer correctly.

Ricky took the Otis-Lennon Mental Ability Test in May 1977, seven months before he was healed. The results were that Ricky was extremely below the tenth grade level, which based on his age he should have been in at this time.

IQ tests and other achievement tests have been shown to be weak in identifying the mentally retarded, the gifted, and in selecting jobs and schools. Inappropriate use of IQ tests has prompted revisions in use for students placed in special education classes. The state of Massachusetts forbids special education students to take standardized tests of various kinds to gain admission to state colleges and universities.

One potential defect in such tests is that the test-taker can accidentally skip a line and then be marked wrong on material to which he or she knew the correct answer. Therefore, most standardized tests are achievements tests and have little predictive value for students, teachers, and schools. They only generate good data for narrow skill sets or topics.

Another weakness of standardized testing is that they do not measure creativity, thoughtfulness, perceptiveness, judgment, diligence, critical thinking, problem solving, and imagination.

Overall, the most fundamental problem with standardized academic achievement tests is that there is little evidence to support the argument that they measure what they claim to measure. The tests have very little relationship to actual academic performance of any kind. Standardized tests scores often measure superficial thinking and were never intended to measure the quality of learning or teaching.

Records show that even in 1977 Ricky was still reading no higher than third grade level before the healing. The same records show that Ricky jumped from special education to the tenth grade. In other words, the records show that at age sixteen, before his healing, he was in the third grade level. After that he was able to comprehend from the seventh grade on up to the tenth grade level.

After the healing, a psychologist consulted with Ricky and concluded that he should be placed in the tenth grade. Before this, according to the psychologist, Ricky had only been reading on the third grade level. In a letter to Ricky's high school, the psychologist wrote, "This young man has been evaluated rather thoroughly in the past by Dr. Ross at Shands Hospital, and has received frequent tutoring in numerous situations." Years before the healing, Dr. Ross had tested Ricky for three days at Shands. This battery of tests included in-depth testing of his brain patterns with electrodes attached to his scalp.

The public school system did not recognize Ricky's serious mental limitations, and they passed him from year to year and from grade to grade, even though he could not read one letter. The statement of Mrs. Young reads, "Ricky was promoted year after year to sixth grade when he reads only on a primer level! He came into special education with no reading ability at all." According to Mrs. Young, Ricky was on a primer level in reading, which is below kindergarten level. How could someone who could only read below a kindergarten level be normal when he should have been in the sixth grade?

The Elementary Standard Achievement Tests that Ricky took after his healing in 1977–78 show an increase overall. Further, the Standard Achievement Test showed that he should no longer be in special education classes since his intelligence had increased from the third grade level to at least as high as the tenth grade level.

The course offerings record shows that Ricky was removed from special education and placed in the tenth grade.

The Stanford Task Test of Academic skills was given to Ricky in 1979, 1980, and 1981. These tests show that he had improved from extremely below average to at least above average and high above average.

In tenth grade (1978–79), Ricky made four A's and four B's. In eleventh grade (1979–80), he made all A's and one B. His senior year of high school (1980–81), Ricky made all A's and one B.

At graduation, Ricky was doing second year college courses, was recognized in the top 90 percent of his high school, and placed at least in the top 90th overall in the nation.

Ultimately, the records that deal with the SAT (or Admissions Testing Program of the College Board) are confused. First, the records show that Ricky made all A's in his final year while he made six A's and one B. Next, the records say that he took in his last year a foreign language. If he took it, it is a mystery to him. Ricky did not take Biological Sciences, or Physical Sciences either in his final year. One part of the records shows a higher score on the SAT than another part reporting on the same test. This is the record as it came to the Roberts' family.

The Facts and Actions Apart From the Records

1. At approximately twelve years of age Ricky was evaluated by University Christian for admittance to the private Christian school. Based on the evaluation conducted by the staff of University Christian and Ricky's public school records, University Christian placed Ricky in a special education elementary school classroom. University Christian's evaluation concluded that after five years of school attendance in the public school

system and at age twelve Ricky was performing at a first grade level academically.

2. Ricky then spent approximately five years under the care and academic guidance of the University Christian special education staff and within that controlled environment University Christian only moved Ricky up three grade levels within the special education program. So at age sixteen, after five years of working with him, University Christian deemed Ricky's progress to be no more than a third grade special education ability.
3. Also at age sixteen, in the middle of his third grade school year, University Christian suddenly moved Ricky out of special education to tenth grade mainstream classes at the school. He immediately became an honor roll student, making nothing less than a "B" on all his report cards, and two years later graduated with high honors.

Common Sense Questions:

A) If Ricky had the ability to learn or if he had been learning over time, perhaps by additional tutoring, why was he not steadily promoted over the five years in the special education program?

FACT: At sixteen years of age, after five years at University Christian School, Ricky was still in special education classes and had only progressed to the third grade.

B) Why would a school knowingly hold back a student for five years if they knew he had the ability to learn? Or why would a school tutor a student instead of promoting him to a classroom where the curriculum would be more challenging to him? This would not only be a disservice to the student, but it would not benefit the school.

C) Why would a school hold a child for approximately five years (age twelve to sixteen, counting age twelve as a first year) in elementary special education classes and then promote him seven grades into mainstream high school classes all in the same academic year? How is that possible or even logical? What prompted the sudden move? What were the reasons behind the decision? Where is it documented? Years in special education: 1973, 1974, 1975, 1976, and 1977.

FACT: Ricky was sixteen and in a third grade special education class prior to the Christmas break. After the break, he was promoted by University Christian to be mainstreamed in the tenth grade.

D) University Christian made the decision to promote Ricky from the special education ELEMENTARY program to mainstream HIGH SCHOOL classes all in the same academic school year. Did the school prepare Ricky for the much more advanced high school curriculum without attending the seven grades in between? (Example: third grade math to high school algebra)

FACT: Report cards show Ricky received all A's and B's on ALL his report cards once promoted to the tenth grade on trial.

E) Ricky had five years' experience and preparation for the elementary version of the SAT, but literally had very little time to learn the information included in the high school version of the SAT. How did the school prepare Ricky for the SAT in order for him to receive the score he did? (Example: One year Ricky took the elementary SAT, the next year he took a high school SAT, without advancing through the grades needed to learn the information tested for in high school.) How is it possible for a student who has taken the elementary SAT more than once and spent five years in elementary school receiving low grades to jump to a brand new SAT with content he has never been exposed to and receive a similar score as the elementary SAT? How is that possible? Certainly, if considered logically, Ricky should have failed the high school SAT since he was never formerly taught the material that it tests.

F) How does University Christian explain or document how a sixteen-year-old third grade special education student, under their instruction, was promoted seven grades all at once and graduated just two years later?

FACT: He was promoted, he was an honor roll student all the years of high school, and he did graduate with high honors.

G) How many other special education students have been instantly promoted several grades and successfully graduated in the top grade point average of their classes at University Christian School? If the school were to get the credit for this success that Ricky experienced, why didn't they duplicate their efforts with other special education students? What made Ricky the exception?

H) If University Christian was instrumental in Ricky's sudden academic success, why did they not document the program they employed to obtain that level of success? Where is the documentation that would be needed to validate such an advance?

I) An intelligence test is not based on any level of academic learning but on the mind's intelligence or ability to process information, reason, learning, etc. so no academic program could increase Ricky's IQ test score. IQ does not change based on education. Therefore Ricky's IQ score documents that he was three points above a moron level—with that low of a score it would be virtually impossible for Ricky to process seven grades of information in one year and pass the testing necessary to advance into the tenth grade, let alone make the honor roll. So how was this accomplished?

FACT: Ricky's IQ score speaks for itself and is further evidenced in his first ten years of education (from age six to sixteen). He was unable to process information at a normal level.

CHAPTER 8

Steps Toward Healing

By a Healed Dr. Ricky Roberts

Several writers of the Old and New Testaments, especially Mark in chapter six of his Gospel, paint a clear picture of how a person can be healed spiritually, emotionally, mentally, and physically. (See Romans 10:9–13.) If a person wishes to be healed by Christ, he must follow these simple steps: know Jesus, recognize a need that cannot be met by man, unashamedly beseech Christ for the miracle, have faith, approach Jesus first, know the hindrances to healing, and know how to obtain and keep a healing.

Step One: Know Jesus

The first step to healing is recognizing who Jesus is. To know Him is the greatest type of faith. Mark says that the people knew

Jesus (Mark 6:53–56). They fully recognized and knew exactly who He was.

They knew Christ by experience. It is undeniable that some had been touched and healed by Jesus. Many others witnessed Him touch and heal friends, strangers, and members of their own household.

The people knew that Jesus was present and reachable. He was available to touch them and make them whole. And they knew that He had the power to make them whole.

Likewise, we must know, as they knew, that Jesus Christ is present, reachable and available to make us whole. He is also able and willing to move for us. This knowledge must include believing that He has "come to seek and to save that which was lost (Luke 19:10); that "the Son of God was manifested, that He might destroy the works of the devil" (1 John 3:8), that He came "that they might have life, and that they might have it more abundantly" (John 10:10) and that He is "not willing that any should perish" (2 Peter 3:9).

Step Two: Recognize a Need that Cannot be Met by Man

The second step to healing is acknowledging that we have needs we cannot meet. There are needs that we can easily fix or meet, but there are other needs for which only God can provide. We cannot take care of all our needs. If we fail to add God to the equation of our lives, we will ultimately fail at everything. The eyes of men are on the earth and on man alone. Therefore, man in his own self is useless and powerless to supply completely what he needs.

Mark says that the people "ran through that whole region" bringing their family members and friends to Jesus (Mark 6:55). They even spread the word about Jesus to strangers. What a picture of people needing something that they could not meet themselves!

And here is also a truth that few realize or notice: the people ran to Jesus, not Jesus to the people. They carried as many as possible to Jesus. Wherever He was, they determined to find Him. If Jesus was not present, they picked up the sick and rushed to the next village, searching for Jesus until they found Him.

Yes! That is a key! We must search for Jesus Christ until we find Him! And we must believe that Jesus can help us, regardless of the outcome.

From this picture then, a true church will be an open church. It will open its doors so that the power of God can heal, deliver, set free, and cast out. A true church provides the opportunity for people to be delivered.

Step Three: Unashamedly Beseech Jesus Christ for the Healing

The third step to healing is beseeching Jesus Christ without holding back and without any shame. Mark portrays beseeching as prayer. Prayer must always begin with repentance. (See Luke 18:9–14.) Prayer must begin with acknowledging that we are sinners saved by grace through faith. While prayer begins with repentance, victorious and overwhelming prayer begins with recognition of God's presence. We must realize that God is present when we pray and that He leans forward to catch even the whisper of those who earnestly seek Him.

To pray effectively, we must recognize that God is as much present now as Christ was present when the people brought their petitions to Him when He was on earth. It is in the recognition of the presence of God that we find it easy to pray and easy to exercise faith. In learning to recognize His presence, praying turns from a chore to a joy and a delight.

True prayer must have God first and everyone else second. (See Matthew 6:10.) Prayer must be done unselfishly for the whole cause of Christ. Praying must be definite. (See Mark 11:24.) And praying is not a means by which we obtain anything that might take our fancy. God has a plan, and we must conform to that plan.

Moreover, prayer must be in the dominion of Christ—abiding in Christ. (See John 15:7.) With every promise in the Bible there are conditions. The promises and the conditions are inseparable. We can ask what we will, and it shall be done only if we abide in Christ and His words abide in us. One of the principles of the kingdom is, "Draw nigh to God, and he will draw nigh to you" (James 4:8). God always hears Christ, and if we abide in Christ, He will always hear us. Conversely, we have the right to be heard only if we abide continually in Him. This is the key to successful prayer. We have to admit that thousands of prayers go up to God that are not answered. Why? Either God does not fulfill His promises, or else those who pray are not fully abiding in Christ Jesus. Faith in God is one thing; obedience is another. The two are tied together. Faith without obedience can only wither and die. True faith requires a conscious, daily submission to the will of God.

In Mark 6:56, we should notice the Greek text and its use of the imperfect tense. The people, according to the imperfect tense, were in a state of asking, praying, and begging to touch Jesus Christ. They repeatedly tried to just touch Him. The people had a sense of need, humility, and desperation. Yet, we give up so easily!

The passage in Mark 6 shows that we must humble ourselves. According to the Greek, there were no "special" people present and none were guaranteed to touch the hem of Christ's robe. Not one was guaranteed a healing. God demanded their effort and faith. The Greek so strongly points out these steps to healing, but it also shows that there is no guarantee to be healed.

For example, my dad was dying of cancer. He was on his deathbed in the hospital praying for people and they were being healed, and yet my father was dying. Though many were healed, my father died. Did he lack faith? No! It was not God's will that he should continue to live.

Step Four: Have Faith

The fourth step is to have faith, which is clearly seen in this passage of Mark. Our faith builds the resolve in us to reach out to Christ so that we may touch Him in the time and place that He desires. Our faith, having Christ as its object, becomes the bridge we use to reach Him. Our faith is so important that, without it, no miracle, gift or deliverance can be received and kept. (See Hebrews 10:35–39 and 11:1, 6; James 1:5–8; Romans 14:23; Ephesians 6:16.)

Commonly, it is said that faith can move mountains. (See Matthew 21:21.) How true! But what if four people are praying about the same subject—the same mountain—yet each desires a different outcome? Indeed, all four people have faith, but how shall God move? Shall God answer four different ways, or shall God answer that which agrees with His will?

All four prayers will not be answered, yet it is not a faith problem. It is a praying problem—praying against the will of God. Therefore, faith can move God only if God wants to be moved and if that faith is tied to His perfect will.

Faith must never been seen as a force used against God. That is not biblical. I know many say that Mark 11:22 should read, "Have faith *of* God." Wrong! God is not a faith being. If that were the case, then someone greater than God would have to exist so that God could trust and have faith in someone greater than Himself. This is not the case. Actually, "Have faith *in* God" is the correct translation. The objective genitive is used in the Greek text and it states that God is the object of our faith; not that God has faith or we can have His faith. The Greek text, regardless of editions, points this out so clearly.

Faith must not be viewed as a formula or as an instant solution to all our problems. Faith comes as a result of a dedicated life and knowledge of the Word of God. Faith only works by the person believing God's sovereignty, power and providence and by lining up one's request with the will of God. Faith alone can do nothing. Faith alone cannot make God do anything. Yet faith in an awesome God can do great things.

In other words, we must learn to unite our will and our faith with the authority of Christ, the power of the Holy Spirit, the will of God, and the sovereignty of God. These all must line up in perfect harmony. Our prayers must also line up with the will of God, God's sovereignty, God's power, and God's providence.

The importance of faith is seen in that without it nothing can be received and kept. (See Hebrews 10:35–39 and 11:1, 6;

James 1:5–8; Romans 14:23; Ephesians 6:16.) Without faith, no promise, healing, prophecy, or deliverance can stand and continue in a person's life.

Faith is activated through a person's speech and especially by their following and doing what God says. (See Romans 10:10; Mark 11:23.) Faith is turned loose in a person's life when they obey God and do what He wants them to do. Through obedience they are taking a stand and literally acting out their faith for some task, deed, or work. Faith brings victory. Faith accepts the goal of God and motivates the people to work.

Faith requires a person's total commitment to a task. Faith is never a leap into the dark. Rather, faith is a leap into the light. When we move by faith, we know where we are stepping, because we are walking in the light of the Word of God.

A great verse about faith that is commonly overlooked is 1 Samuel 17:37. It adds to the passage of Mark so well here. This verse reads, "David said moreover, The LORD that delivered me out of the paw of the lion, and out of the paw of the bear, he will deliver me out of the hand of this Philistine. And Saul said unto David, Go, and the LORD be with thee." In this one verse, we are told the classic story of faith. If there were no other passages about faith, this one would be far more than enough for us to understand genuine faith.

Faith *reacts* to the challenges, obstacles and blasphemies of evil against the will of God. (See 1 Samuel 17: 23–27.) The story of David and Goliath is an example of this. Goliath was standing in God's way. There was no way around it; Goliath had to go somehow. David's faith would not allow him to stand in silence while Goliath defiled God. Faith stands with the will of God, works according to His will, and reacts to anything or anyone which becomes a hindrance to His will.

In 1 Samuel 17:28–32, we see that faith *resolves*. David ignored his brother's condescending remarks and pushed forward with purpose to defeat Goliath. A person with genuine faith makes their mind up to do something regardless of the price. For a healing, there is a heavy cost. And few want to pay that cost.

In 1 Samuel 17:34–47, we see how faith *remembers the victories of the past*. Saul challenged David's ability, saying he was just a boy and incapable of defeating the mighty warrior Goliath. David remembered the lion and the bear he defeated in the past. He told Saul, "Thy servant slew both the lion and the bear: and this uncircumcised Philistine shall be as one of them, seeing he hath defied the armies of the living God" (v. 36). In times of sickness, distress, trouble, and tribulations, faith remembers the things the Lord has done. This strengthens one's faith to hold on for the promise at hand.

Verses 37–47 reveal that faith *relies on God* Who will never fail. David acknowledged God's intervention in his battles, saying it was "the LORD that delivered me out of the paw of the lion, and out of the paw of the bear, he will deliver me out of the hand of this Philistine" (v. 37). When we are in trouble, we must recognize and depend upon God. The essence of genuine faith is that it looks to God as its object.

Finally, faith *receives*. (See 1 Samuel 17: 48–51.) In David's mind, before he ever stepped out on the battlefield, Goliath was already dead and buried. The instant David placed the battle in God's hands, faith won the victory.

Truly, we need an obedient attitude, an attitude that believes and follows Jesus. Conquering the impossible requires great faith, and often it requires standing all alone against everyone else. My father and mother stood alone for years holding on for my healing. You may say that they had "stubborn faith." Stubborn faith is the type of faith that desperately denies self in order to seek Jesus no matter the cost. Above all, parents should have stubborn faith when it comes to their children. They must refuse to give up when others have already given up.

Step Five: Approach Jesus First

The fifth step is to remember that in times of sickness, torment, troubles, and disaster, Christ usually will not approach us unless we first approach Him. (See James 4:8.)

Even the greatest of men and women must approach Jesus begging, totally dependent upon Him. There is no other way. Position, rank, power, fame, wealth, social status and social acceptability must be laid aside. Our thoughts cannot be focused on ourselves. We must focus only upon Christ and His power if we wish Him to meet our need.

Therefore, when we do draw near to Him, we must do so with confidence, humility, and reverence, like the leper did in Matthew 8:2: "And, behold, there came a leper and worshipped him, saying, Lord, if thou wilt, thou canst make me clean." The leper should be our example of how to approach Jesus and how to receive from Him.

In Matthew 8:3, we see it is Jesus' nature to respond to our requests for healing: "And Jesus put forth his hand, and touched him saying, I will; be thou clean. And immediately his leprosy was cleansed." How wonderful it is when you sense Him saying to you, "I am willing!" Matthew tells this story so we can know that Christ possesses both the ability and the willingness to heal us of our illnesses.

It is important to note that how we approach Christ determines the outcome. Often, our behavior, attitude, and motive are wrong. Therefore, before we approach Him for anything, especially healing, we must humble ourselves and check our behavior, attitude, and motive so that we may receive His favor. We may need a change in these areas before He will move.

Further, in Mark 5:21–23, we see three main ways to approach Jesus: the desperate approach, the hopeless approach, and the believing approach. The most important of these is the believing approach. This approach always lays hold of Jesus. Jesus knows when a person truly believes. This approach involves one simple attitude or act. There is neither fear nor despairing attitudes in faith. Believing has nothing to do with fear or despair. There is not a wailing, whining attitude in faith. Believing has nothing to do with such an attitude. The answer is Jesus' comfort and assurance.

Step Six: Know the Hindrances to Healing

The sixth step is knowing the hindrances to healing and trying to prevent them in our lives. There are many hindrances that will stop or keep God from moving in our direction. Our ignorance is no excuse. We need to know the hindrances, repent, and work at rooting out such things that will keep us from being healed.

God does not fall short; we fall short. We fail to grab hold of all that God has for us because we set limits for what we believe

He will do. When the Holy Spirit enters a pı does not come to heal just one thing. When I perform healings, miracles, deliverances, blessings, and many other things that we cannot imagine.

Knowing the hindrances to healing is the first step in rooting them out of our lives. They are listed as follows:

- Wrong motive (James 4:2–3)
- Doubt (Matthew 11:23–24)
- Praying against God's will (1 John 5:14)
- Iniquity in the heart (Psalms 66:18)
- Refusal to hear God's law (Proverbs 28:9)
- An estranged heart (Isaiah 29:13)
- Sinful separation from God (Isaiah 59:2)
- Waywardness (Jeremiah 14:10–12)
- Offering unworthy sacrifices (Malachi 1:7–9)
- Praying to be seen of men (Matthew 6:5)
- Pride in fasting and tithing (Luke 18:11–14)
- Lack of faith (Hebrews 11:6)
- Asking wrongly to spend it on selfish passions (James 4:3)
- Inconsideration of husband or wife (1 Peter 3:7)
- Lack of understanding the Word of God (Hosea 4:6)
- Lack of understanding what a new creation is (2 Corinthians 5:17)
- Lack of understanding one's place in Christ (1 John 4:4)
- Lack of understanding righteousness (James 5:16)
- Lack of understanding our right to use the name of Jesus (Acts 2:38; 3:6)
- Not acting upon the Word (Matthew 4)

- Satan stealing the healing (John 10:10)
- The person not being thankful or not giving testimonies about the healing (Luke 17:11–17; Ephesians 4:17; 3 John 1:3)

Step Seven: Know How to Obtain and Keep a Healing

Many years ago, I heard a minister speak about healing among the people of God. His conclusion was absolutely horrible. He said that 90 percent of the people the Lord heals lose their healing shortly thereafter or over time. Why? Was it their fault? Did they have no faith? His conclusion was based upon one scripture: "The thief cometh not, but for to steal, and to kill, and to destroy: I am come that they might have life, and that they might have it more abundantly" (John 10:10). The minister believed that as these people left his crusade, Satan was there waiting, trying to steal their healing, miracle, deliverance, promise, blessing, or whatever else God had done for them.

I also have seen this happen repeatedly over my many years of public ministry. One case disturbs me even to this day. It disturbs me, in many respects, because of what was lost, how it was lost, and the horrible results that followed. Satan never reminds me of all those who have been healed, but he loves to point out those who were not healed, or those who lost their healing. It is hard for me to keep count of those whom God graciously healed that I personally witnessed, but Satan will always come around and point out those who lost their healing or deliverance.

I remember, many years ago a teenage girl was suffering greatly from brain tumors. The whole church prayed for her, and the power of God came upon her in a glorious manner. She knew that she had been touched by the hand of God. I told her that she must live for God and honor Him by following His moral commandments. A few days after the prayer service, she went back to the doctors, and they could not find any tumors. The doctors were utterly dumbfounded. Right before their eyes they had proof that God had moved. And did He! But then Satan moved, like he was playing a game of chess, or like a commander on a battlefield. What destruction followed I will never forget! By the time I was brought into the situation the tumors had come back with a fury and killed her. Satan stole her healing.

What was the sin that caused her to lose her healing? First Corinthians 6:13–20 speaks about fornication and its evilness. She threw away her healing just because she wanted to have sex with two boys in the backseat of a car. She threw away everything that God had given her just for a few sexual pleasures. Everyone should think about that for a minute or two!

God warns of the consequences of sin. Galatians 6:7 reads, "Be not deceived; God is not mocked: for whatsoever a man soweth, that shall he also reap." And some consequences of sin cannot be reversed as seen in this case.

I have heard too many times that once God heals, He heals, and you do not have to worry about losing it. Wrong! Ignorance, stupidity, sin, and disobedience can cause you to lose your healing, besides the hindrances already discussed. All Satan needs is a doorway, and there are myriad. Once I prepared a teaching on the many doorways we can open to Satan. I stopped counting at a hundred. There were many others that followed!

In the New Testament, when a healing, miracle, deliverance, or exorcism is mentioned, the aorist tense mostly is used. Grammatically speaking, this points out that the person received some type of complete and often instantaneous miracle, healing or deliverance. However, the tense does not indicate whether the people kept their gift from God or lost it. It is possible that some kept it for a time or for their whole life. It is also possible that some lost it immediately, or kept it for a short time and lost it. The use of the aorist tense is a warning that what is gained from the Lord may be lost.

There is another example that Satan brings back to my remembrance; one which I'm certain I will never forget as long as I live. I still weep for what was lost. There was a young man that I met many years ago who was trying, with little success, to recover from drug addiction. He had tried all kinds of addiction programs, but they failed.

His background was terrible. He started on the road to destruction by selling drugs, but never using them. He thought the people who bought drugs from him were dirt, trash, stupid, and utterly ignorant of the consequences that follow that kind of life. He carried a shotgun in his car and $50,000 petty cash. This young man was being blessed; not by God, but by Satan himself. Everything was going his way. He had women, money, cars, and more success than most young people that age could have or handle.

A day came when Satan set a trap against him. Up until this time, the young man had never taken any of the drugs he sold. However, Satan played this young man well. The young man walked into a crack house to do business. The main dealer over the crack house had a simple rule: you must take crack cocaine in front of him. If not, you were dead. Crack cocaine is known to be instantly addicting. From that first experience the young man became a heavy drug user. Everything Satan had given him was taken away.

This young man had become such an influential drug dealer that the local and federal authorities were looking for him. Finally, Satan pulled his protection from him and he was arrested. His future expectations were gloomy and ghastly. Years of prison time stretched before him. Yet, God through His grace began to make His move. The extensive prison sentence disappeared, and the young man received only a short prison time and many years of probation.

The first night he came to our service, I had no idea who he was or what he had done, but the Lord knew. The church began to pray for him. We all were crying out unto to God for him and invoking (calling upon) the anointing of God to come down and deliver him. At the end of the night I did not know what or if anything had happened to him. All I knew was to pray regardless of the outcome.

The next week a new, godly young man appeared before me, completely delivered of drug addiction. For years, God moved for this man. God removed the heavy length of probation. God even erased his criminal record, as I understood from the young man, so that he got a very good job. Within months at his new job he was running the store as a manager. God continued to bless him so much so that he was able to open his own stores.

But Satan is always there waiting in the wings. Satan is the 300 pound gorilla in the room that no one wants to speak about. He is ever vigilant, watching for a door to be opened so that he can come in and bring his hellish misery upon people.

The bottom line is that the young man ceased being close to God, refused to come to church, divorced his wife, and moved away from where he lived. I knew what was going to happen. I saw the wreck before the crash. The last time I talked to him, I beseeched him not to throw everything away, not to reject God by returning to the destructive lifestyle he once had. He refused to listen to me. The last word I received about him was that he died from an overdose in a crack house. The sorrow I feel over this young man returning to his own vomit cannot be measured in words.

There is a gentle, gracious and merciful side of the gospel, but there is equally a fixed, just and judgmental side. The gospel is unchanging. If we take one part out, it is no longer the gospel. If we add to the gospel, it is no longer the gospel. It is complete and perfect in its own right. While there is the blood-stained Lamb in redemption, there is also the Lion of the Tribe of Judah. Countless men and women will pray at the last day to be delivered from His wrath.

It is a dreadful thought that a time can come in this life when God rejects a man. More than once I have witnessed Christians enjoy divine favor and honor, and then they begin to wander astray. They fall deeper and deeper into sin, in spite of all that God desires to do for them. At the last, anyone can see that the Lord gives them up.

Accordingly, I teach those who attend True Light Ministries to bind all their healings, miracles, deliverances, blessings, and whatever else they believe God is doing or will do in their lives. I urge them to continue in faith and obedience, lest something worse fall upon them!

What does it take to receive and keep a healing?

- Remain and continue in Christ Jesus (1 Jc [illegible]:24–25).
- Remain and continue in the Word of the Lord (John 8:31).
- Continue in the love of the Lord (John 15:9).
- Continue in the grace of God (Acts 13:43).
- Continue to be sold out to God, and to walk and live the faith (Acts 13:48; John 3:16).
- Continue in the goodness of God (Romans 11:20–24).
- Continue in the faith—grounded and settled—and be not moved away from the hope of the gospel (Colossians 1:22; Titus 1:1; Romans 8:24–25; Acts 14:22).
- Continue to look into the perfect law of liberty (James 1:25).
- Keep the commandments of God (John 15:9–10).
- Continue in prayer (Colossians 4:2).
- Continue in the doctrine of the gospel (1 Timothy 4:11–16).
- Continue to reject unbelief (Romans11:20–24).
- Do not walk in the sins of the past life, living that life again (Luke 8:13; 1 Peter 3:11; Ezekiel 18:21; John 8:11; Ephesians 4:22).
- Persevere and endure all things for the prize of unconditional security and unconditional salvation (Mark 13:13; Matthew 24:13).
- Live in the very state of obedience to holiness, grace, and all that for which God stands (1 Peter. 1:2; Acts 6:7; 2 Corinthians 6:9).

- Do not commit any death penalty sin (Ezekiel 3:17–21; 18:4–29; Romans 1:21–32; 1 Corinthians 6:9–11; Galatians 5:19–21).
- Do not be removed from Christ, nor fall away from grace (Galatians 1:6–8).
- Do not provoke God to anger or tempt Him with utter contempt (Matthew 4:7; Luke 4:12; Romans 1:24–32; Hebrews 3:16; Ezekiel 8:17; Ezekiel 16:26).
- Do not refuse to hear, to obey, and to follow Christ (John 10:27–29).
- Make things right when sin is committed (1 John 1:9; 2:1–2; James 5:19–20).
- Do not allow Satan to steal the healing (John 10:10).
- Continue to be thankful and give testimonies about the healing (Luke 17:11–17; Ephesians 4:17; 1 Corinthians 15:57; Psalm 102:1–5; 3 John 1:3).

O Lord, I pray that all bow their knees to the God of the miraculous and find out just how powerful He can be. And I pray that they will keep what God has given them and never allow Satan to take it from them.

VERBUM IPSE DEUS

CHAPTER 9

Ministerial Impact

God did not heal Ricky Roberts just to improve Ricky's quality of life or to make his parents happy. In the Gospel of Luke we are warned, "For unto whomsoever much is given, of him shall be much required" (Luke 12:48). Dr. Roberts' life is dedicated to study, prayer and ministry. In 1999 the Lord prompted him to begin True Light Ministries in Jacksonville, FL, and Douglas, GA. During weekly prayer services at both locations, Dr. Roberts prays for the spiritually, mentally and physically sick. Countless miracles and deliverances have occurred at these special services where God's power, glory and anointing have been poured out upon the people. Below are only a few examples of True Light Ministries' impact on people from all over the world. Please note, the testimonies have been lightly edited (only changes made to improper spelling for clarity sake), so as to retain the original authors' voices.

Teen Healed of Learning Disability

I came to church for prayer Thursday night, Pastor was praying for me and saw in the Spirit a light, and then I saw the light and he was talking about how it was a light for my knowledge and my comprehension to increase. The next day I went to school and I started reading and I understood everything that I read. Normally it would take me four or five times of rereading, but that day I understood it the first time. I was able to do homework, a whole packet in under 20 minutes, which normally would take me about 2 hours to complete.

7-Year-Old Boy's Emotional and Sensory Issues Improving

My son Luke, now 7 yrs old, is a child that showed signs of being on the Autism spectrum, although never diagnosed officially. After many conferences with teachers and counselors, the conclusion was that he has social anxiety and sensory issues. I was desperate for help for him, and willing to put him on medicine if that was how God wanted to heal him. His anger and outbursts were frequent, he would not look you in the eyes, he would have meltdowns over simple changes to his routine and he would have to be "peeled" off of me when I would drop him off for Sunday school. Any changes in his routine would set him off. Academically, he's ahead of his level, and specifically he is 2 years ahead in reading. His teacher, who has years of experience with special needs kids, said that he's brilliant and will more than likely be shy all of his life. She's been great at helping him and has a lot of wisdom and understanding concerning him. At times, I felt like I could not handle his outbursts, and all I could do was just cry and pray. He's physically strong and sometimes would start hitting me as well. Once he would start in a meltdown/

tantrum, he could not snap out of it and it would just spiral out of control. Many times, he would tell me that he was sad and he didn't know why. I continued to pray, ask God for wisdom, tons of grace and healing for him. Last summer, I received a prayer cloth that had been beautifully covered in prayer and anointed. Without Luke's knowing, I placed the prayer cloth inside of his pillow. I would continue to pray over him and break every tie that binds and bless him with peace and God's healing. Now, 8 months later, Luke is intentionally giving me hugs, looking at me in the eyes and making sure he tells me that he loves me, all things that he would not do willingly before. He now tells me that he's happy or that it's been a happy day. At church, they don't have to "peel" him off of me as often, as he is willingly taking their hand walking into the classroom. He feels secure at church, at school and at home now. He loves more now, and has found joy deep inside, laughs more and smiles all the time. I know that it's all for God's glory that my son is now pulling out of this and being set free. He has a calling, he's smart and has a lot of love to give, and he now has confidence that he didn't have before. Yes, there are still times that he may start to have a meltdown, but now he's able to snap out of it and control his frustrations. He's progressing greatly. During this time, he has not been on any medication. He's healed and continues to be healed, and I know that only by God's hand is this possible.

Soldier Healed of Shattered Bones and Brain Damage

In 2008 a family member of a soldier in Iraq came to a service at True Light Ministries. The soldier had been hit by an IED in Iraq and suffered shattered bones and brain damage. His cousin and aunt asked Dr. Roberts to pray for him. After prayer the family received word that the soldier was completely healed of the shattered bones and brain damage. Doctors were baffled.

Nephew, 19 years old, tanker, deployed to Iraq, less than 3 months

Thursday Morning Phone Call (17-Jan-2008)

Hit IED – explosion so massive, ejected him from tank

Hit head on lid, causing traumatic head trauma, unsure extent of brain damage.

Every bone in both legs and feet were completely shattered

Broken back w/multiple spinal column/cord fractures

Ruptured Spleen

Placed in medically induced coma

Listed in severe/critical condition with life threatening injuries

Thursday Evening/Late Night

Went to Ricky's service originally for prayer for my son

Son requested prayer for cousin (nephew) instead...said cousin needed it more

It appears, within minutes of prayer over son for nephew, doctors started pulling him out of the coma (to assess brain damage)

Approximately 1 – 1 ½ hours after prayer phone call from doctors to wife

No apparent brain damage, nephew spoke to wife and seemed himself (upset about iPod getting blown up...LOL)

Was to be placed back in coma and transported immediately after call to Germany

Early Friday Morning

Blood detected in abdomen, kept off plane for another assessment

Bleeding from spleen, doctors felt safe to fly and have surgery in Germany

Found after rerunning and performing additional tests EVERY BROKEN BONE in his body WAS WHOLE AGAIN! Only injury was hyper-extended knee!

Once in Germany

Headed for pre-op testing for spleen (MRI, etc) and other internal injuries

Doctors spoke with nephew's mother and stated the following:

Found minor injury/trauma to the 9-12 vertebrae, no fractures

Performed MRI, repeated it and other tests

Quote from Doctor "There is NO medical explanation, we have tested and retested, but it appears that your son's SPLEEN is HEALING ITSELF!"

Chemical burns on chest, arms and back

Suffering severe PTSD (we will continue to pray healing for this)

Arrived at Ft Sam Houston in San Antonio, TX on Tuesday morning (22-Jan-2008) to receive treatment for the burns.

From A. L,

Child Healed of Tumor Behind Eye

Dr. Roberts and Dot Roberts prayed for "Jeffrey," asking God to remove a tumor that was behind his eye. Doctors were planning to remove his eye, but God had other plans. The tumor disappeared and Jeffrey was able to keep his eye.

Dear Dr. Ricky,

Thank you very much for your prayer. God had answered your prayers and performed miracles. Last night when Tom told me that the Hospital had called asking us to bring Jeffrey in today, immediately I knew that it must be you and your mother who had prayed, so God reinstated the appointment that I previously cancelled. This is Miracle #1.

Miracle#2—This morning at the hospital, the specialist checked Jeffrey eyes under anesthesia and he did not see the tumor that the other doctor was talking about. So he does not need to do an operation to remove Jeffrey's eye. Jeffrey got to keep his right eye!! Thank you, Jesus, Halleluiah!!

Please continue to miracles for Jeffrey:

Thank you very much again. Please send my best regards to your mother. We love her.

Chronic Inflammation Healed and Dissolving Shoulder Muscles Restored

In 2006, I met with an Orthopedic specialist seeking a diagnosis and treatment options for impairment of my right shoulder, where eight years earlier I began to have pangs of pain followed by limitations of movement. Gradually my condition worsened until I reached the point of feeling unbearable pain and experiencing extreme movement limitations. At touch, my shoulder felt hot and appeared to have twisted in the socket. After an examination with an Orthopedic specialist, tests were ordered, and a diagnosis was rendered. The Dr. told me that I had a condition that was seen in only 1% of their patients. The pain in my shoulder was caused from chronic inflammation, so severe that it dissolved my shoulder muscle tissue into a taffy- like condition. The weight of my arm had pulled the shoulder muscles into a thin and stretched state much like the pulling taffy, which led to my shoulder ball dropping and tilting in the socket. All of this explaining the symptoms causing the progressive increase in pain and limitations of arm and shoulder movement.

Furthermore, there was nothing that could be done medically, so the Dr.'s advice was "to learn to live with this condition."

For the next year I tried suffering through the pain and making the necessary changes in my daily routine to care for my husband and children. The fact that I was right handed meant that many many tasks requiring physical labor were left undone.

Finally, I could live this way no longer, and realized that this was an extreme problem that called for an extreme solution. After assessing my options I knew that I had to do one of two things, look at the possibility of amputation, or seek God's grace for healing.

Having heard of a local minister who was reported to have healing take place at his services, I sought out True Light Ministries for prayer through Dr. Ricky Roberts. The first night that I attended his service proved to be a life changing experience. God revealed himself to me in multifaceted ways that night, but for the purpose of this testimony, I will only center on the aspects of my healing.

First, Ms. Dot came and prayed for me, breaking the many curses that had been hindering my life and then offering me words of encouragement. As she did this, I saw the glory of God around her and felt truly loved by her. Later Dr. Ricky came and talked with me and prayed for my healing. Immediately I witnessed - what I now know to be the Shekinah Glory of God - a pure golden colored beam flowing through the minister and in through my core, penetrating into the innermost part of my being. The Love of God was all encompassing, pure, powerful, and was simultaneously feeding the starvation of my soul, healing my heart, giving me new knowledge and uplifting me in all ways. He especially took the time to show me just how special I truly am to Him. Next, God revealed to me that Dr. Ricky is truly a pure man and His holy servant, and that this was the kind of minister that I had searched my whole life to find. After prayer, I went back to my seat and began to feel the muscles being massaged in my right shoulder. Upon noting that no human being was touching me at the time, I knew that I was experiencing a supernatural act of God. Over the next two weeks God continued to work on me until my arm was healed. God then called for me and my family to become a part of True Light Ministries' team where we continue to serve God to this day and to truly understand what it is like to live blessed.

A Woman Delivered of Evil Spirits

I started attending True Light Ministries (TLM) in December 2012, only on Thursday Prayer meetings. I was attending another Church on Sunday and Wednesday. I was attending TLM weekly and continued at the other church where I was teaching Sunday school and Wednesday youth group. It was in March of 2013 I missed a Prayer Meeting at TLM because I was participating in Jail Ministry with the church I was attending. My plan was to go to the TLM in Douglas, GA on Sunday. I told no one at the church but my husband. While in church that Sunday morning a woman stood up behind me and spoke in tongues and then said in English, "Daughter do not go, if you go you will perish, Have I not given you children, have I not given you grandchildren? If you go you will perish." I went Home and paced the floor, asking God, do I go do I not go? I went. That was not a message from God through this woman behind me as you will see.

In that service at TLM in Douglas GA, Pastor Ricky prayed that God would give me wisdom. I sat on the floor; I tried to get up but could not. Screams started coming from me, People were surrounding me rebuking, and praying, and Pastor Ricky commanded the thing out of me, it was a battle. Pastor Ricky was fasting; it was the eighth day of his fast. This started the beginning of my deliverance. By the following Thursday when Pastor Ricky prayed for me all evil spirits were cast out. (And He said unto them, This kind can come forth by nothing, but prayer and fasting. Mark 9:29)

I found through TLM I would have gone to Hell if I had died, I was not saved. No one knew I was possessed with evil spirits. Not my husband of 25 years, not my friends at the church who were witness to my water Baptism 5 years earlier and who all were attending TLM, not even me. You may question why after attending TLM for four months, was I not delivered earlier? To everything there is a season, and a time to every purpose under the heaven: Ecclesiastes 3:1, only God knows. I have since been attending only TLM and am abundantly Grateful to True Light Ministries and to God who has raised up this man Dr. Ricky Roberts, healed him, anointed him and appointed him over this ministry. I attended several other churches over five years and none of them had the Power to set me Free. If the Son therefore shall make you free, ye shall be free indeed. John 8:36. I am indeed free!, and my life has completely changed, it is no longer my own. Praise God.

True Salvation and Deliverance from Alcoholism

A wife and mother shares how God transformed her life at True Light Ministries from knowing about Jesus to true salvation and having a relationship with Jesus Christ. She makes the distinction between being a "Cultural Christian" and being a true sinner saved by grace. God delivered many members of her family from illnesses and one from severe alcoholism. The miracles in her life were all a result of consistent prayer and attendance at True Light Ministries.

I've been attending True Light Ministries for almost two years now, and in that time God has recreated me and my family. Though the

Lord has worked many miracles and deliverances in our family over these few short months, the greater miracle I cannot deny is the true conversion of my soul. I have considered myself a Christian my whole life...raised in the church by God-fearing parents. And yet, I didn't know Jesus. In all that time of attending church and "doing" my religion, I never gained a full understanding of who Christ is, much less developed an interactive and meaningful relationship with my God.

Seemingly endless factors played a part in my spiritual failure (including a healthy portion of rebellion on my part) and yet I thought I was fine and right with God. I turned a blind eye to how closely my life resembled the lives of the blatantly unsaved around me. God in His mercy pulled me up out of the pit I truly was in and He helped me see that my commitment to my relationship with Christ resembled a twig house built on sand. I realize now that I was, to use Patrick Morley's words, a "Cultural Christian." I mixed cultural norms into my faith and thought nothing of it. The problem is, a little leaven leavens the whole loaf, and the worldly standards I accepted in my lifestyle contaminated my faith and weakened it to the point that I was powerless to fight against a major attack from Satan. The Bible teaches us that sin weakens the hedge of protection God places around us: "He that diggeth a pit shall fall into it; and whoso breaketh an hedge, a serpent shall bite him" (Ecclesiastes 10:8).

And powerless is exactly how I found myself when I darkened the door of TLM for the first time (though I had visited the church a few years prior). It was a Sunday morning and I was at death's door (as many people seem to be when they come to True Light for the first time), fresh out of the ER from the Friday night before. Satan had attacked my heart, and I almost died. But God is merciful and He used my weakened physical state to strengthen my spiritual man.

Through the teachings and leadership at TLM the Holy Spirit began rebuilding my foundation on the rock of Jesus Christ—and I have watched in awe as I have truly changed from the inside out. It's been an interesting start to a journey that I pray will never end. Miraculously, I didn't try to change, and yet it happened. He changed me—God's precious Spirit. The worldly things that never used to bother me grieve my spirit today. I can see now where all the "Church" rules come from that, in my youth, seemed (to me) to stifle people and make them feel unaccepted in the church unless they "cleaned up" their lifestyle. These "rules" must come from people who totally surrendered to God and were transformed by His Spirit and then they turned around and tried to force their heart-changes onto others who had not yet experienced the same process of sanctification. We can do nothing to set ourselves free...it is Christ's Spirit working in us that sets us free!

When I fully surrendered to the Holy Spirit and asked Him to transform me into the image of Jesus, He began stripping away my desire for and acceptance of things that I didn't realize were separating me from a deeper walk with God—things that, in His eyes, blended me in with the rest of the world. Before I knew what hit me I found I couldn't wear half of my old wardrobe to church; the thought of standing at the altar and pouring my heart out to the Lord in some of my outfits made me shudder. Of course God would accept me "as is"...but He was changing me and teaching me what pleases Him—and some of my old "norms" had to go. This is just one small example pulled from a mountain of proofs. The beautiful part is that the change I experienced was effortless; meaning it didn't come from me. I'm the kind of person that if you tell me not to wear something or not to indulge in something, I'll do it just to irk you and make sure you know you don't control me. So this change was coming from somewhere else—and it amazed me! What happened? I still am awed by the influence of the Spirit in my life now. I tested it out with an old movie that I used to love to watch. It's a harmless comedy—centered on drug addiction (nice, right?)—and it always made me laugh. I put the movie on a while back and after about twenty minutes I couldn't watch it. I was uncomfortable; it wasn't funny this time around; and I literally felt sick to my stomach. I had to shut it off. Physically sick? I can't fake that. It was the convicting power of the Holy Spirit reminding me to be careful what I set before my eyes.

Since I made TLM my home church and have followed the teachings there, I have proof in myself that the Lord is working in my life. This has not been a painless process—Satan has instigated full-on attacks against me and my family and we have suffered physically and emotionally. I have also silently watched as many of my friends and family have pulled away from me into the shadows and background of my life. They see the changes in me now too, and many of them, I believe, are not sure what to think—so they stay away. I think of how David must have felt when he wrote these words: "Because of all my enemies, I am the utter contempt of my neighbors; I am a dread to my friends—those who see me on the street flee from me. I am forgotten by them as though I were dead; I have become like broken pottery" (Psalm 31:11–12).

To be abandoned by loved ones and friends is considered disastrous by most people's standards, but for me it is all the more reason to rejoice! It is proof that I have changed. It is proof that God's anointing is upon my life and that He's using me to influence others for His glory. I have His peace. I have the contentment of knowing for certain that I am running the race and I'm contending for the prize—no longer am I sitting on the sidelines while the battle rages on. I have stepped into the fight; I've accepted the call to be a part of the "chosen generation, a royal priesthood, an holy nation, a peculiar people; that ye should shew forth the praises of him who hath called you out of darkness into his marvelous light" (1 Peter 2:9). By doing so I've been awakened to the reality of spiritual warfare and the fury of Satan, our accuser, toward God's saints. When we are willing to surrender to the Lord and become a slave of Jesus Christ, Satan zeroes in on us and focuses his efforts on destroying us. The Bible tells us to "be sober, be vigilant; because your adversary the devil, as a roaring lion, walketh about, seeking whom he may devour" (1 Peter 5:8). He's not seeking after his own—he already has them under his thumb. This verse is referring specifically to the blood-bought saints—the Christ-centered warriors who are sacrificing life in this world to bring glory to Jesus Christ. I pray now that the Lord keeps me under the shadow of His wings that He keeps me from the fowler's snare. Father God, let me never again fall back into Cultural Christianity. Keep me set apart; a drastic and offensive contrast to this wicked world—ever moving forward on the path toward Your marvelous light.

Other miracles in my family resulting from prayer at True Light Ministries:

1. *I was scheduled for heart surgery and one week before the procedure was to take place my insurance refused to pay for the surgery. My husband and I took a step of faith and went forward with the procedure (after months of prayer, we knew this procedure was God's will). Though we were risking being hit with $100K worth of medical bills we decided to trust God to defeat Satan's attack against us. During my surgery my husband was called down to the hospital's offices to pay a $20K down payment on my surgery. He talked them down to $10K, swallowed hard, and wrote the check. The very next morning, while I was recovering in the hospital bed, the insurance company called and said they put my case through another director and the procedure was approved for full coverage. Over the next six months the Lord led us through battling for this coverage—Satan was*

still trying to steal our miracle. I prayed daily for six months for our $10K check to be returned as well. God is faithful and one Saturday morning, out of the blue, I opened yet another "medical" envelope and found my refunded check! As of today, all medical bills related to this surgery have been paid in full. Greater is He that is in us than he that is in this world!

2. *A loved one was totally delivered from alcoholism and has kept it. The smell of alcohol makes this person sick. They say it smells like rotting flesh to them now. This is someone who drank every day—all day. God mercifully delivered them during a Thursday night prayer session at TLM. By Friday morning they were clean and sober without having to go through withdrawal symptoms or any sickness. They haven't even had to struggle with temptation. The Lord completely erased all desire for alcohol from their mind, will, emotions, and physical system.*
3. *My cousin's newborn baby was suffering from lung problems and was totally healed. The child was in intensive care in a hospital in Texas. We prayed on a Thursday night for the child and the baby was home and doing well a few days later.*
4. *My 2-year-old son was suffering from 104-degree fever for four days. The fever would not break, even with medicine. The doctors offered no solution other than Motrin and Tylenol. We brought him for prayer on a Thursday night and around 1am Friday morning I heard him screaming in his room because he was drenched with sweat—the fever had finally broken. He was perfectly well by morning.*
5. *My four-year-old son was suffering from violent nightmares that would hit every night at 10pm. After consistent prayer in the TLM prayer line and having him sleep with anointed handkerchiefs the nightmares have disappeared.*

6. *My husband suffered from unexplained abdominal pain for over ten years. He went to every specialist imaginable—even spent time at Mayo Clinic for testing—and no one could figure out what was causing the pain. Dot and Ricky Roberts prayed for him throughout these long years and today he is completely set free from the debilitating pain.*
7. *My husband also had a rare condition where his jaw bone was growing up through the gums, causing excruciating pain. Sharp bits of bone would break through the gums and crack off in bits and pieces. The dentist said there was nothing he could do—just live with it. My husband went for prayer on a Thursday night and the condition ceased. No more bone fragments—no more pain. Praise God!*
8. *My husband was suffering from tinnitus (ringing in the ears). Doctors said there is no cure and that he would just have to get used to the ringing. There are reports of people actually going insane from this condition. He came to TLM for prayer on a Thursday night and the ringing completely stopped. No problems since.*
9. *I had a painful lump in my left breast—came for prayer at TLM and then went for a mammogram. No lump could be found.*
10. *My father-in-law was suffering from a back injury. He came for prayer at TLM on a Sunday morning. Dot Roberts prayed for him, and the back pain was completely gone by the next morning. He had been to the doctor and gone through physical therapy—nothing was helping the pain. God delivered him through His great mercy!*
11. *When we first began attending TLM my small children were afraid of the prayer services. They didn't know how to handle all they were feeling as the presence of the Holy Spirit would*

flood the sanctuary. I prayed diligently that God would calm their fears and that they would someday be comfortable enough to come down for prayer. The Bible says that "the fear of the Lord is the beginning of wisdom" (Psalm 111:10). Today all four of my children are at peace in TLM's sanctuary and they look forward to Pastor Ricky praying for them. I remember one Thursday night I was blown away as my daughter sat on the second row, coloring a little picture, while a demon was being cast out of woman five feet in front of her. My daughter was in total peace; she didn't even look up. God has transformed my babies over the past two years. Discipline problems have lessened and honest discussions about Jesus and our faith abound on a daily basis in our home. My children are hungry for more of the Lord. They have some spiritual wisdom that I didn't acquire until I was an adult. They pray in the name of Jesus and trust God for the things they need. When a prayer doesn't get answered, they respond, "Well, it must not have been God's will. We need to make sure we pray God's will next time!" They have a love for Jesus that inspires me to cling more and more to our Father in heaven. I know that He is keeping all of us under the shadow of His wings.

Boy Healed of Abdominal Migraines

A mother's son is completely healed of debilitating abdominal migraines at True Light Ministries.

At 18 months old Nathaniel started having bouts of severe nausea and vomiting that appeared to come in cycles every 60 days and would last 2 days. At his 2-year check-up the doctor suspected that he had Cyclic Vomiting Syndrome. This is a rare illness characterized by bouts of severe nausea and vomiting that comes in cycles. It is also known as abdominal migraines. The confirmation of this illness is one of exclusion. They had to rule out every other possible illness first. This involved him going through 15 different diagnostic tests. Some people have various triggers, but for Nathaniel it was a matter of days, we could mark our calendar for when the next episode would hit. When the episode would happen it would occur during his deepest sleep and he would wake up screaming in pain. Over the years the different neurologists tried many different preventative medications. We also went through many different medications to try to help him through the episode, including some used to help chemotherapy patients, but none of them worked. The doctors finally allowed us to put him on Valium, as it was the only drug that would relieve his suffering. There were many visits to the ER for dehydration due to vomiting as much as 18 times in one night. Over the years he had also suffered from dizzy spells and head migraines in between episodes which caused the doctors to put him on a daily medication. As of July of this year the episodes were running around every 85 days and lasting 1 day. A week after the episode on July 15th we visited True Light Ministries. Dr. Roberts prayed for Nathaniel, breaking generational curses. He also identified and prayed against a specific demon that was oppressing him. Since then Nathaniel has not had any symptoms at all. In September, after seeing his neurologist we were able to take him completely off his daily medications. It has now been 120 days since the last episode. He has never gone this long. To God be the glory!!! We have taken Nathaniel to be prayed for many times by many different pastors. Until Dr. Roberts prayed for him, no one had ever prayed for Nathaniel to be delivered from demonic oppression. Words cannot express our thanks to God for this miracle. It is wonderful to know that Nathaniel can sleep peacefully without the constant threat of this illness. We praise God for the way He is working in Dr. Roberts and the ministry at True Light.

Woman Healed of Calcium Deposits in Breast

A woman came to True Light Ministries for prayer over calcium deposits in her breast that doctors feared might be cancerous. A biopsy confirmed that no cancer was present.

Dear Ricky:

I want to thank you for the wonderful gift you are to the body of Christ. A year and a half ago I was told that I had calcium deposits in my left breast. The doctor recommended that I have surgery to remove them and that a biopsy was going to be made. Of course a woman hears this and panic sets in.

I was fortunate enough to ask you for prayer. You did just that and informed me that these calcium deposits could turn into cancer but GOD had healed me as you were praying. The next day I had surgery. All the calcium deposits were removed and a biopsy was expected. The surgeon felt that everything looked clear but the biopsy would confirm that. After a week the results came in. No cancer was found in those calcium deposits, GLORY TO OUR GOD. The surgeon, however, mentioned that the report indicated that my breasts were prone for cancer. I immediately called you to let you know that MY GOD HEALED ME BEFORE I WENT INTO SURGERY.

I live with a grateful and thankful heart to the Lord for His blessings in my life.

Again, thank you for your obedience to the Lord and for praying for me.

Open Heart Surgery Cancelled and Heart Healed

My testimony the Pastor just preached, because name is Anna. I came here believing God for prayer. My friend told me this is a place that believes in prayer. This is a place that REALLY believes in prayer. Some people pray, but they do not really believe that God will do what we ask. Pastor prayed for me and mother [Dot] prayed for me. I was here because August the 12th I was scheduled to have open heart surgery. When I was born I had an incomplete mitral valve that didn't completely finish forming as it should. Therefore all my life... I didn't know I had this problem until I was about 50 years old, and then I was diagnosed. So the mitral valve had been replaced in 2010; and then the doctors told me that it had to be replaced again. I am 73 so I was very concerned about having the surgery again. Two doctors had told me "Don't have it... If it's not bothering you, don't do it. The surgeon at another hospital where I had another opinion said, "It's best to have the surgery while you are healthy so you can go through the healing." Well God... I came and put it on Him, and I was prayed for and I was told that "God's going to do a Rotor Rooter on your heart." And I didn't know what that meant. All I knew was God said He was going to do it. And I took that [Word] and I kept that... I was in the hospital all of August, because every time they thought that they had finished, they found something else. So it came back to me: "Rotor Rooter." They sent me home, and then I had to come back because the rhythm of my heart was not what it should be. And they wanted to put in a pace maker and all of that. I still believed that God had this. He gave me a scripture as well: "No weapon that is formed against thee shall prosper." And these weapons just kept coming, but in the end I knew that God had me because that was what I was told here: "That you are in God's hands; He loves you, and He has you, and He's going to do a Rotor Rooter. So I put myself in God's Hands and walked with the Lord; let the Lord walk with me. I'm here tonight because this Monday they were to do another procedure on me to get my rhythm right. Normal rhythm is 72. Mine was 151. And they had given me a shock treatment. That didn't work. So now they said, "We're going to go in your heart through the groin and we are going to do an electrical charging of your heart, and that part of your heart that's sending out bad signals, we're just going to burn that part." I'm sure you've heard of that before being done. And I go into the hospital at 11 o'clock on Monday. They were supposed to do this procedure at 1:00. Well, they didn't come to me to do anything. They kept coming back and doing EKG's and coming back and doing EKG's... Finally my doctor came in and said, "I need to tell you something that's good news." And I said, "What?" And he said, "What we saw before we don't see any more." I said, "What do you mean you don't see anymore?" He said, "Your heart is in rhythm. We don't have to do what we thought we were going to have to do. Now the Lord took me through all of that, and everything is documented now. It's documented that I had it, and it's documented that it's gone! I am with you because I appreciate the love and the prayer, but I wanted to give God the glory for this.

Woman Healed of Diabetes

In the beginning... years ago... I was teaching a class on forgiveness. And my friend said, "You have to go to the doctor." And I said, "No." We checked my blood sugar and it was 1,369, and I landed in the hospital. I came out having to take insulin shots. Dr. Ricky has been praying for me for me on and off for years about a divine, creative miracle for the pancreas to be healed and everything. The last time that they checked it, it was PRE-diabetic... And I haven't been pre-diabetic in THIRTY years! :) So God really did heal this incurable disease, and I'm glad to share it. I'm so thankful for the prayers here. They have been a blessing!

72-Year-Old Woman Healed of Dyslexia

I thank God for the opportunity tonight to tell you what a wonderful God we serve. I was here last month on the second Thursday of the month... Virginia and I came up from Melbourne because she had loaned me the book that she was talking about, and I read the book [A Walk Through Tears]. She said, "Do you want to go?" [to TLM in Jacksonville] and I said "yes," and so I came... And I just want to thank God for Virginia and for this ministry because on that Thursday night I sat in here and worshipped with you people. And then after the pastor came up to pray for people, I came up. And Virginia couldn't figure why I was coming up for prayer. She said I got up and I shot to the front... Because you see, I'm seventy-two years old, and my whole life I've had a problem, and I could not conquer it, and I did not know that it could be conquered. But after reading that book, I said, "If God can do that for the pastor, He can do it for me!" And so I came up...and I'm dyslexic... And so I came up and he prayed for me. And he knocked me out... God knocked me out on my fanny; and I stayed out for a while.

Now I can read better and I can do things that I could never do before that! Praise God! Thank you so much for this ministry! God bless you all!

A Walk Through Tears and TLM Blessing for Family

I just finished reading this book for the 4th time. I will probably read it many more. I found this wonderful church 10 years ago and it continues to bless my family in countless ways.We have experienced healings, miracles, deliverances and encouraging prophetic words to stand on and pray in.We have learned the meat of the scriptures and how to intercede to see our prayers answered.We are so blessed and honored to be taught and pastored by Dr. Ricky Roberts and Mrs. Dot Roberts.

Stroke Symptoms Healed

Wife:"I was standing in my bedroom and I felt something like a sharp object going through my temple, and the left side of my face didn't feel the same. And I knew that I had had a mini or slight stroke."

Husband:"To God be the glory... When Dr. Roberts prayed for my wife last night she instantly received a miracle and all the symptoms were gone. To that we give God all the glory and praise!"

Wife:"I don't have that pain in the eye area anymore ...[after the stroke] I had a hard time remembering or putting things together; I would have to think... And I notice now that my thoughts are flowing... it's like they are free-flowing. Beforehand I was forgetting everything. I'm beginning to realize now that I'm beginning remember more. I'm thankful I was able to come down [from NC] and be with this awesome pastor, and his mother and this church family. I was told that when I came down that God was going to heal, and that's exactly what He did! I'm going back different than when I came!"

Man's Vision Restored, Surgery Not Needed

I was having problems with my eye. September the 6th I was supposed to be going out to Shands [hospital] to have an operation on my right eye. When the pastor was praying, I'm looking at the pastor, and I couldn't hardly see him. My eye was jumpy and was blurry. So, I was squinting *trying to look at him. So he put his hand over my eye—and I looked at him. I said, "Look at there! I can see! The Lord healed my eye!" I said, "Lord Jesus... all these years I've been going through this. They're talk about going into my eye for the fourth time; he put his hand on my eye and healed me just like that!" I said, "This CANNOT BE NOTHING BUT THE LORD HERE!"*

93-Year-Old Man Healed of Back Pain

The second time I came down [to TLM in Jacksonville] I got prayer for chronic lower back pain. I had the pain for quite a while... I'd say several years. I asked Ricky to pray for me for that and he did so. I was slain in the Spirit. When I got up off the floor I realized that my lower back was not hurting me anymore. All the way home in the car [St. Simons Island] I was testing it out and it felt better. I say, "Thank you, Lord, for what You did through Mr. Ricky." Mr. Ricky didn't do it. God did it. I believe God is the Great Healer.

Ruptured Discs in Lower Back Healed

I was diagnosed last year with two ruptured discs in my lumbar spine, and tonight when they prayed for me... I don't feel any discomfort back there at all. So PRAISE GOD! I also came for healing from hives. I think that God just did a number on me tonight! I think He just worked on EVERYTHING!

For healings and miracles to take place like this, the minister has to pay a heavy cost for the authority of Jesus Christ and the power of the Holy Spirit in his life. Indeed, the minister has to consecrate and dedicate his life more than others to the Lord.

He has to forgo what most people want for the Lord, and throw his all unto the Lord. He becomes in many respects a slave unto the Lord for the sake of the church. He has to be a pure vessel since God refuses to allow the authority of Jesus Christ and the power of the Holy Spirit to be used by a unclean vessel. In essence, such a minister must have the four things that God truly and absolutely honors: simplicity, purity, obedience, and faith. If Dr. Ricky Roberts did not have these, the Lord would not move at True Light Ministries, and many of the pages of this book would be blank.

As you can see, this ministry has never lacked the authority of Jesus Christ and the power of the Holy Spirit. What we have lacked is a continuing and growing stream of people standing with us—like-minded people—and a continuing and growing stream of funds. **Think of standing with us!**

For more information concerning Dr. Roberts, his mother, their schedule of events, their ministry and donations to the ministry, please contact:

True Light Ministries
P.O. Box 28538
Jacksonville, FL 32218
A Non-Profit and Tax-Exempt Organization
Phone: 904-281-1411
Fax: 904-751-0304
www.truelightministries.org

ENDNOTES

Introduction

1. Tertullian Against Marcion, 5:15. Own Translation.

2. John Wesley, The Works of John Wesley, 10:23.

3. Jonathan Edwards, The Works of Jonathan Edwards, 1:375.

4. Ibid, 2:261.

5. Thomas Kyd, The Spanish Tragedy (London: Nick Hern Books, 1997).

6. Marie Shropshire, God Cares About Your Tears (Eugene, OR: Harvest House Publishers, 1997), 147.

7. A. W. Tozer, God Tells the Man Who Cares (Camp Hill, PA: Christian Publications, 1992).

8. Marie Shropshire, God Cares About Your Tears, 10–11.

Chapter One
Beginnings of a Miracle

1. Cordelle Dispatch, May 2, 1918.

Special Education 1973-1974

Special Educational 1975

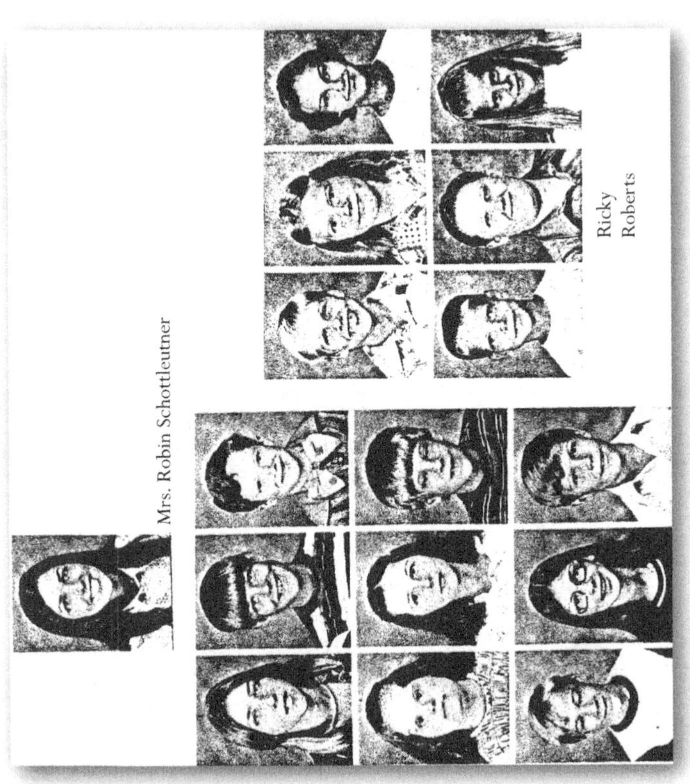
Mrs. Robin Schottleutner
Ricky Roberts

Grade
Spec. Ed
teacher
Mrs. Dugger

SOPHOMORES

March 27, 2000

To whom It may concern,

I knew Dr Ricky Roberts as a retarded teenage, was present the night God healed him and saw personally the after effects of such a healing.

Sincerely, Maggie Kim Carver
and daughter
Ruth L. Chambers

Reading level

1st 9 wks. – Pre primer level Book 2

From the back of the first report card in Special Education: This indicates that Ricky Roberts was reading below kindergarten level, although being 12 years old.

Made in the USA
Las Vegas, NV
17 January 2023

65809240R00105